I0824453

# RELEGATED

## Also by Todd Smith

*Brave Enough*

*Hockey Strong*

# RELEGATED

**One American's Pints-and-Pies Journey from the Top to the Bottom of English Football**

Todd Smith

**GALLERY BOOKS**

New York Amsterdam/Antwerp London
Toronto Sydney/Melbourne New Delhi

G

Gallery Books
An Imprint of Simon & Schuster, LLC
1230 Avenue of the Americas
New York, NY 10020



First Gallery Books hardcover edition May 2026

GALLERY BOOKS and colophon are registered trademarks of Simon & Schuster, LLC



Interior design by William Ruoto

Manufactured in the United States of America

10 9 8 7 6 5 4 3 2 1

Library of Congress Control Number: 2025937803

ISBN 978-1-6680-6676-8
ISBN 978-1-6680-6678-2 (ebook)

Some names and identifying characteristics have been changed.

*For Sass*

# CONTENTS

Contents

The United Kingdom
The Isle of Lewis and Harris, Outer Hebrides, Scotland
Atlantic Ocean
Stornoway, Isle of Lewis and Harris, Outer Hebrides, Scotland
Greater London
Tottenham Hotspur Stadium, North London
London Borough of Newham, East London
Westway Sports & Fitness Centre, North Kensington, West London
Craven Cottage, Fulham, West London
Scotland
Arbroath, Scotland
N
W
E
S
North Sea
Northern Ireland
Sugden Sports Centre, Manchester
Stockport, Greater Manchester
Isle of Man
Goodison Park, Liverpool
Grimsby Town, Northeast Lincolnshire
Wrexham, Clwyd County, Wales
England
Wales
Nailsworth, Stroud District, Gloucestershire
Bristol
Bath
Somerset
Brighton and Hove, East Sussex
Celtic Sea
English Channel

# INTRODUCTION

## Minneapolis

I was baptized into the sport of soccer during the raucous days of the North American Soccer League (NASL) when my dad, Gary Smith, was the head athletic trainer of the Minnesota Kicks. In the late seventies, the NASL was a traveling circus. Fans went to rowdy, beer-soaked tailgates and postgame rock-and-roll concerts. The players were primarily foreign born, with the United Kingdom being particularly well represented, and because of this, I was immersed as a child in British football culture.

I would tag along with my dad to work and roam freely through locker rooms and practices. I picked up slang like "dodgy" and "cheeky." Places like Blackpool and Nottingham Forest and Stoke-on-Trent that I'd read about in the Minneapolis library were brought to life by the players talking about their former professional clubs. When the Kicks went to England for training and exhibition, I went, too, visiting the old grounds of English football—great fortresses of steel and concrete and fencing, where the matches were sodden and scrappy and my dad's training room came to look like a wartime triage tent.

My favorite Kicks player was a gent from Cambridgeshire named Mike Bailey. Bailey wasn't as popular as some of the starrier NASL imports like Pelé, Franz Beckenbauer, Johan Cruyff, and George Best, but he was a legend in his own right, a bruising midfielder with the roguish good looks—heavy muttonchops included—of a swashbuckling pirate. Known as "a hard man," a tough tackling butcher who patrolled the midfield looking for legs to chop down, he'd been the championship-winning captain of the Wolverhampton Wanderers back in England in 1974. Bailey was Robert Plant's favorite player, and during a Led Zeppelin concert at the Kicks' stadium in 1977, the singer shouted him out. In my impressionable eyes, no one was cooler than Mike Bailey. Because of him, I became a Wolverhampton fan early on in life and have stayed that way ever since.

Inspired by Bailey, I became a soccer player myself. I played year-round from a young age, evolving into a runty and mouthy left-footed left back with the physicality of a honey badger. I was a three-year starter on my high school's varsity team. Meanwhile, the NASL folded in the mid-eighties, but my dad took a job as head trainer of a new team called the Minnesota Strikers, who played in the Major Indoor Soccer League. My first job was as my dad's locker room attendant, so I spent nights and weekends in the company of the players—these included the English-born Alan Merrick, Kenny Fogarty, Allen Willey, Steve Litt, and Brian Kidd.

I went on to St. Mary's College in Winona, Minnesota, an NCAA Division III college where I was on the soccer team for one year. A year later, I transferred to the University of Montana and left my soccer-playing days behind. I was crispy with burnout from playing and training year-round for close to a decade and sought refuge in the cool trails and mountains of the West. After graduation, I led a nomadic existence, living in Hawaii and Los Angeles and New York City, and only dabbled in pickup games but nothing serious. I eventually returned to Minneapolis and fell in love with my wife, Sarah, got married, and started a family when our son, Murphy, was born. When Murph was a baby, life was simply too busy for a proper kickabout.

Though I was no longer a soccer player, my love for the sport didn't fade. It just turned into an obsessive, couch-based fandom. Every weekend from September to April, the house I shared in South Minneapolis with Sarah and Murph filled with the roar of supporter chants and songs on the TV. In addition to watching the English Premier League—widely considered the top soccer league in the world, and indisputably the wealthiest and most watched—I began keeping tabs on some of the lower-league teams that I'd heard about from the Kicks and Strikers players.

As much as I appreciated the skill of the top players, over time the British towns and fan bases I found myself relating to more were the scrappier ones that filled the many lower divisions. I loved stories of perseverance and courage in the face of staggering odds (my dad was also the head athletic trainer for the 1980 "Miracle on Ice" United States men's hockey team, ahem), and I became obsessed with the unique structure of relegation and promotion that can mean death or survival for teams without billionaire owners. The English football system, which has been in place since at least 1898, "promotes" the top few teams in each division and "relegates" the bottom few down to the next division. For a smaller-market team, moving up to a higher level of the game can bring life-changing money that boosts the local economy, the job market, and a town's identity. The reverse can have devastating ripple effects.

It wasn't hard to determine why I related to the lower-level teams. You see, as much as I dreamed of being a wealthy, prize-winning writer—a Manchester United of literature, let's say—that fantasy never really came together for me. I was more of a Wolverhampton of literature, a bruised and calloused writer toiling in the lower leagues with occasional flashes of glory. I've published two books, one a nonfiction story about ice hockey and one a memoir that I helped Olympian Jessie Diggins, a cross-country skier from Minnesota, write. I've also been a sports journalist and a magazine columnist. But I've never made much money or gotten much recognition from my writing. Instead, I've spent my career in the Twin Cities landscape and gardening industry.

For the past five years, I've been the director of a landscape supply yard called Hiawatha Supply, where we sell soil, mulch, and rock in bulk. I spend half my days driving heavy machinery and the other half managing the business side for the company's owners. Before Hiawatha Supply, I managed another supply yard, and before that, I worked as a day laborer at a garden center, and before that, I toiled in a grocery store dairy cooler, and before that I worked in various warehouses. My occupations have given me a happy, humble, quiet life, but always nagging in the back of my mind has been a case of impostor syndrome. I've felt like I never really made it as a writer.

Then, in 2021, I was given the opportunity through a connection at *The New York Times* to submit an essay about a local organization I'd started six years prior called the Donkey Soccer League. Organizing the league had brought my sporting life back into the present tense after a two-decade hiatus. It felt great to play again, albeit badly. We were no longer the thoroughbreds of our youth and had resigned ourselves to being beasts of burden. But what kept me and the other out-of-shape dads and assorted middle-aged nitwits coming back every Sunday, year-round, was the brotherhood we formed. As aging soccer players, we had tapped our collective histories with the game to grab something that most adults had lost along the way: a love for the golden art of pickup soccer. More important, my fellow Donkeys included immigrants from Ireland and England and various South American countries. Donkey soccer was our reprieve from the weight of the world and the foundation of an unlikely community during a time when political forces were trying to build walls between us. That's what I wrote about in my essay.

As I waited to hear back from the editor, I couldn't help but acknowledge how much getting published in *The New York Times* would mean to me. I fantasized that if I could just see my byline in the same place as those of my writing idols—Dan Barry, John Branch, Rory Smith—I would finally have made it.

Then the piece was rejected. In the nicest rejection email ever, the editor told me that the essay was "perfect as-is" but it was simply too long. "And we don't see any place to make cuts to it to try to make it fit." As kind as that sentiment was, my confidence was cratered. The experience nearly broke me—it felt like confirmation that all my dreams were dead. By this point, I was nearing fifty, and I wore the scars of working outdoors. My fingers had been smashed and cut and blackened so many times I'd lost count. I had early onset arthritis in my hands, feet, and shoulders. A growth on my eye—the result of chronic sun exposure—was slowly squeezing my vision. But with writing feeling like less of a career option than ever, continuing to run the supply yard seemed to be my only choice.

For the months that followed, I kept writing here and there, but without much drive. I watched sports. I ambled my way through Donkey League games. I did my job at work, and grilled chicken for Sarah (who hated to handle raw meat), and helped raise Murph (who was nearly done with high school). But I was teetering dangerously close to a sad-sack midlife crisis.

That's where I was at, mentally, in 2022, when I found myself watching an English football match between Premier League giant West Ham United and the Kidderminster Harriers, a lower-division club that I'd never heard of before. The match was part of the 2022 FA Cup tournament, the oldest national football competition in the world. The magic of the FA Cup is that it is open to all eligible clubs from the Premier League all the way down to the lowest level of the English football system. This creates true David-versus-Goliath scenarios, matches between the best teams in the world and those on the very fringes.

At the time, West Ham held fifth place in the Premier League and was battling for a spot in the vaunted Champions League, a yearly competition for the top club teams in all of Europe. Kidderminster, on the other hand, was in the National League North, six tiers down. The match was played at Kidderminster's tiny Aggborough Stadium and not at West Ham's sprawling one in London, where the opening and closing ceremonies of the 2012 Summer Olympics had been held. This meant an English Premier League club worth $1.1 billion had to travel by coach to the town of Kidderminster, which resided on the edge of obscurity, sandwiched between Shatterford and Stourport-on-Severn in the country's Midlands region. Instead of playing in front of sixty-eight thousand spectators, they had to play for three thousand.

Kidderminster led 1–0 from the nineteenth minute to the ninety-first. I was mesmerized by the images on the TV. Supporters were spilling over each other in the stands and pressed up against the railings, sauced and sweaty and singing and cheering their boys on. The Kidderminster players had day jobs and worked as plumbers and lorry drivers in their spare time, and they were going toe-to-toe with West Ham's world-class players. In the corner of the screen to the side of one of the goal lines was a food truck, where a grizzled man in a soiled white chef's apron smoked cigarettes while taking a break from serving meat pies. This was about as far from the glitz and glamour of the Premier League as I could imagine, and I absolutely loved it.

In the last seconds, West Ham's Declan Rice, an elite English midfielder who would go on to sign a record-breaking contract a year later with Arsenal for £105 million, tied the match with a thumping shot that exploded into the Kidderminster goal. With the game knotted at 1–1, the match went into extra time. West Ham's Jarrod Bowen, a magically shifty winger, scored the winning goal in the 120th minute (or "at the death," as it's known in English football parlance). It was a heartbreaker.

After the game, the Kidderminster Harriers and the valiant fight they'd shown kept tickling at my brain. There was something there that wouldn't go away.

I casually opened my laptop and typed in the team name.

And I fell down a rabbit hole.

Kidderminster was home not only to a football club but also to a "Museum of Carpet." According to a newspaper poll, the team sold the best meat pies in town at their home matches. There were teams in their division named Kettering Town and Leamington and Spennymoor Town. I read about the Wycombe Wanderers and the Dorking Wanderers and the Stockport County Hatters—real names, to my delight and awe. *What is the worst city in England?* I asked Google. Apparently, it was a decimated former fishing port appropriately named Grimsby. *Was Boreham Wood a real team or the greatest porn star name ever?* They were somewhat disappointingly a real team and not a porn star and were currently in a real dogfight with a club from a place called Slough Town. I searched and read and searched some more. I envisioned myself in these places. I couldn't get enough.

When I was done and the screen's glow faded, I was struck by a new sense of purpose. I didn't want to be three thousand miles away from where the sport I loved most was invented and obsessed over in every region of the country. I wanted to go there. I wanted to attend matches in the grand cathedrals of English football and in the tiny stadiums nestled in the nooks and crannies of factory towns. I wanted to meet the characters who inhabited those worlds. I wanted to sing the songs. I wanted to press against the sideline railings. I wanted to go to the pubs and roar through the night. I wanted to be a part of a football-mad tribe of locals in a place where nothing mattered but the game at hand.

I wanted to eat the meat pie.

The flicker of my old writing ambitions sparked to life. I asked myself, *What if I wrote a travel memoir about one American rube's journey through the world of English football?*

Not long after that day, Sarah came home from her job as a cashier manager at a garden center and saw the giant map of the UK that I'd affixed to the kitchen wall with painter's tape.

This new purchase marked the names and locations of more than 150 football teams. They sounded like mystical places from a Tolkien adventure. There was Chippenham Town and Cheltenham Town, York City and Yeovil Town, Havant and Waterlooville, Dagenham and Redbridge. There was Bonnyrigg Rose, Dulwich Hamlet, and Dumbarton.

The front side of the map had all ninety-two football teams in the top four divisions—the Premier League and the three tiers collectively known as the English Football League: the Championship, League One, and League Two. On the reverse side were the locations of the seventy-two teams that make up the first three divisions of the National League System, which sits below the English Football League. Despite the National League having the word "league" in its name, the teams that form its many, many divisions are commonly referred to as "non-league." In simple terms, this means they're only semiprofessional or amateur in status—though in the highest of the non-league divisions, the National League (singular), that's not usually the case. So yeah, it's wonky. But to put it simply, there are ninety-two teams in the top four divisions and more than fifteen hundred in all the divisions below that—which includes the three that were on my map (the National League, the National League North, and the National League South) and then approximately thirty-three others.

When Sarah's eyes moved from the map to the paper piling up in my writing nook marked with the chicken scratchings of a madman, her eyebrows arched to the highest point eyebrows can arch. She knew better than anyone what this mess meant.

"I'm kicking the tires on a book about English football," I confessed. "I'm thinking it might be a travel memoir where I visit teams all over the UK from all different divisions."

Instead of shooting down my harebrained idea, she continued to be the most golden person I've ever met, the human embodiment of the good vibes and bouncing beat and sweet guitar licks heard in the opening chords of the Grateful Dead's "China Cat Sunflower." She had seen me wrestling with my writing demons. She just had a few stipulations.

"I get it. It makes sense. This book is the one you're meant to write. But can you wait until Murphy is in college? Can you wait a year? We need to see how much college is going to *really* cost," she said.

All good marriages are simply a long conversation. When your partner is a creative person toiling away as an artist, that conversation is typically a tangled knot of hearts and minds and money and desires and needs and space and time. The balancing of finances and work and creativity has been part of our life since our first date.

"Yes, for sure," I said. "I can wait."

"I know the writing has been hard for you lately. I know you've really been struggling," Sarah said softly. "And I know you've contemplated quitting. Out of all the other nonsense you've written and out of all the ideas you've conjured up, this one is inside you. Go on and tell this story. But just so you know, I really enjoyed having you around the house *not* writing a book for the last few years. I enjoyed having a functional husband."

"Me too." I laughed.

"I will only ask you to do three things for me as I reenter my role as the Writer's Widow," she said, using a term of her invention.

"First, you will have to grill chicken for me every Wednesday and Sunday."

"Fair."

"Second, you're going to have to move this map and all this writing shit to the basement. I can't live with it in my kitchen."

"Fair."

"The third thing is: Can Murph and I come with you for part of the trip? He can do soccer stuff with you, and I can do anything but that. Lord knows there aren't a lot of benefits to being a Writer's Widow. But this could be really fun."

"Deal!" I said.

For more than a year and a half, I planned and saved up. I mapped out a tentative train route through the UK, one that would take me—and Sarah, and Murph, and other friends and family members at times—from Premier League stadiums to pitches in the corners of the United Kingdom, places where teams kept holding on and coming back to play each week, seeking elevation to the next tiers of football and life.

My long, cold period of feeling relegated as a writer was over. I was promoting myself.

# First Leg of Trip

## CHAPTER ONE

# Tottenham Hotspur Stadium, North London, January 3 & 5, 2024

I stood with Murph at the pinnacle of English football. Specifically, 153 feet in the air on a small glass walkway that extended off the roof of the Tottenham Hotspur Stadium in North London. To our left was a chasm funneling raw, blustery winter wind and beneath it 62,850 empty seats around a gorgeous emerald-green pitch. To our right was a fifteen-foot-tall golden chicken. The statue—of a cockerel, to be precise—has been the Hotspur's emblem since the team was founded nearly 150 years ago.

I had thought it would be poetic if I started my odyssey here, but now that I was looking down, all the poetry in my mind and body was gone. The only thing I was taking in were my testicles, which were climbing up into my stomach in a state of sheer terror.

Worse still, an alarmingly young and motor-mouthed tour guide was a few feet in front of me and Murph. His jibber-jabbering was so constant, and so loud in order to be heard over the wind, that it seemed like he was narrating my rising panic attack.

"In front of us is THE BEST STADIUM . . . IN . . . ALL OF ENGLAND . . . TOTTENHAM HOTSPUR STADIUM! YEAH! LOOK AT IT!" the tour guide said with the excitement of a chipmunk on cocaine. "WE ARE NOW . . . forty-six-point-eight meters above the pitch . . . on the DARE SKYWALK. YOU DID IT . . . Isn't this AWESOME?!?"

In addition to me and Murph, there was a young man and woman on the tour, remarkably on a first date. All of us were harnessed to the railing while wearing mandated jumpsuits and weird grippy black shoes. Sarah, allergic to all things sports, enjoyed her alone time in cafes, shops, and museums.

It meant a lot to me that my lanky, nineteen-year-old son was with me during his last week of winter break from the University of Minnesota. Football was a big part of our relationship. When he was fourteen days old, Murph had heart surgery to fix the coarctation of his aorta, a congenital defect. Then, when he was five, he started suffering from episodes of severe vomiting, migraines, and lethargy. After a year of terrible uncertainty that marked our family's life, he was diagnosed with the last thing we expected: anxiety.

A doctor explained that Murphy was a healthy, sweet little boy with adult-grade panic attacks. With a program of therapy and medication he got vastly better. His sunny personality returned and he did well in school, but the anxiety and migraines remained something he, Sarah, and I had to learn to live with. Initially, sports seemed too challenging an environment to put Murph in, but when he was seven, we decided as a family to try out soccer. The team dynamic, in which he could work with other players and not be alone in the spotlight, was a draw. He liked it, but from his early days of playing, one of Murph's biggest fears was having a panic attack or a migraine during a practice or game and not being able to find Sarah or me. So I decided to be there, in his sight line, every single time he stepped onto the pitch. Initially I was his team's coach. Later, he played on some extremely intense clubs, and I'd drive him to every practice and game. We enjoyed being part of club soccer together. (We also became connoisseurs of post-game frozen ice cream treats.)

Eventually, though, the intensity of the travel club experience chewed us both up. We were tired of driving an hour and a half each way to suburban sports complexes with addresses like "Lake Hill Lane Court East Circle West" that would tie our GPS in knots, to face teams with names like Thunder Academy and Fusion Elite. The other parents would be clad in visors, wheeling buggies full of chairs and umbrellas and coolers and snacks to claim the sidelines. It was all a bit ridiculous in the way that only competitive youth sports can be, and shortly before starting high school, Murph decided he'd had enough of the grind.

Our soccer obsession didn't go away, though—it just found a new form. Together, we became mega-fans of the TV show and then podcast *Men in Blazers*. It was hosted by two British-born American transplants in tweed jackets, whose intelligent, irreverent, off-the-cuff football commentary was so far outside the boring lines of normal sports journalism we could barely believe it. The hosts, Roger and Michael, would mix references to John Cusack and Betty Friedan with analysis on corner kicks and set pieces. Watching and listening to them was a beloved weekly appointment for me and Murph, and the vernacular of the show became our love language, a reference to "*Kummerspeck*" ("grief bacon") or a player named "Jonjo" (who looked like Voldemort) being a way for us to lighten the mood and say I love you to each other without having to actually form the words.

Thus, we found ourselves clinging to the Dare Skywalk together, staring up at the statue of the cockerel. Murph had come to England not only for fun and because he's a good son but because he knew that this entire trip was about more than the book I would write. It was a celebratory victory lap for our family. We were all healthy and happy, and he and I still had a bond, in which English football played a major part.

"Look closely at the football that the . . . GOLDEN COCKEREL . . . stands on!" the tour guide screamed. "DO YOU SEE IT? LOOK CLOSELY! DO YOU SEE THE DENT IN THE FOOTBALL?"

The giant gold football that the giant gold bird stood on did indeed have a dent. It looked like an asteroid crater.

"This statue is a replica of the original . . . GOLDEN COCKEREL statue . . . that was at our former stadium . . . THE . . . LEGENDARY . . . WHITE . . . HART . . . LANE," the tour guide said. "The story goes that back then . . . one of our star players . . . a gentleman you may have heard of named . . . PAUL GASCOIGNE!!!! Old GAZZA HIMSELF . . . WHAT A LEGEND . . . Gazza was out shooting pigeons at . . . WHITE . . . HART . . . LANE . . . and had a rifle and shot at a bird and missed and hit the original statue and the bullet or pellet or whatever it was dented the ball!"

The wind kicked up. I didn't know if I'd heard correctly.

"Did you say a player was . . . hunting birds with a rifle . . . in the old White Hart Lane stadium?" I asked.

"YES . . . GAZZA . . . WHAT A LEGEND! When . . . THE SPURS . . . made this replica for the new stadium . . . THEY MADE SURE TO PUT THE DENT in the ball of the replica . . . as a nod to our past, a sign of the history of the BEST CLUB IN NORTH LONDON!"

God damn, I thought, a berserk player shooting your club logo is a strange thing to be proud of.

"GAZZA WAS A WILD MAN!" the tour guide reiterated.

"Gazza was also a terrible drunk," the young man on the date said to us over his shoulder.

The tour guide kept talking up the team's history and the magnificence of the new stadium we were standing on, which he said boasted a Michelin star–level restaurant, an on-staff wine sommelier, and a cheesemonger. When at last we made our way to the final section of the skywalk, we posed for a picture at the designated spot. The golden cockerel statue and the stadium were the magnificent backdrop.

I took a deep breath. The weight of the entire journey that lay ahead of me suddenly became a reality. This photo was to be the first documented step of my trip. On the first leg, I would spend a month and a half going around some of the biggest and smallest cities in England and Wales. Then I would return to Minneapolis and my day job for about a month, before returning to the United Kingdom for leg two, spending close to three weeks abroad, splitting my time between Scotland and England. Across both legs, I was scheduled to travel through a myriad of football levels and leagues as far south as Brighton and as far north as the Isle of Lewis and Harris in Scotland. I was also set to *play* football all over the UK via an app called Footy Addicts, a social platform that helps people play in organized pickup games in the UK, a fool's errand of the highest order. The photo made the trip, and the book, seem real.

"ONE . . . TWO . . . THREE . . . SPURS!" said the tour guide as the camera fired off a flurry of pictures.

When the photo session was over, the guide came up to the group and said, "OKAY . . . WHO WANTS TO RAPPEL OFF THE EDGE OF THE STADIUM?!?"

"What the heck?" Murph blurted.

"You've done THE . . . DARE . . . SKYWALK . . . now your next adventure is THE . . . DARE . . . SKYWALK . . . EDGE! You can now rappel . . . OFF . . . the side of the stadium!"

He wasn't kidding. He walked us over to an area where people in harnesses were being lowered face-first off the stadium.

"Should we do it?" the young man said to his date.

"Aww . . . aww . . . Yes?!" the young woman said, stuttering seductively.

"HOW . . . ABOUT . . . YOU . . . TWO?!?" the guide then asked me and Murph, absolutely jazzed. "Do you two want . . . TO . . . DO . . . THE . . . DARE SKYWALK EDGE???"

"We'll take the stairs," Murph said.

"My man," I said, as we bumped fists in solidarity.

Two nights later, Murph and I were on our way back at the stadium to see an FA Cup match between Tottenham and Burnley. We'd traveled together to Soldier Field in Chicago to see Manchester United against Paris Saint Germain in 2015, and to the Los Angeles Coliseum to see Manchester City against Real

Madrid in 2017, but those were "friendlies"—the matches hadn't really mattered to the teams. Now we were about to see a third-round match of the FA Cup: the oldest national football tournament in the world, with real stakes!

When we got off the London Overground train at the stadium, I fought the reflex to reach out and hold Murph's hand. We were in a sea of people—exactly the kind of situation that made him anxious when he was younger and that my paternal muscle memory was hardwired to protect him from. But I checked myself. I stepped back, and watched him navigate his way through the crowd, shoulders back, chin up, eyes focused, the rightful hero of his own story. His name, which means "Warrior of the Sea" in Irish, seemed fitting.

Tottenham Hotspur Stadium was lit up in purple for game day and seemed to be levitating, like a spaceship ready for launch. The stadium, designed by the same firm as the Sphere in Las Vegas, is covered with thirty-five thousand decorative metal and glass panels that form a shimmering exterior veil. Though we weren't going to any of them, Murph and I had heard about the stadium's many amenities: luxury suites, wine cellars, a bakery, a microbrewery, a Formula 1–sponsored go-karting track, and the largest team merchandise store in Europe. It also has the longest stadium bar in Europe, and *that* seemed worth a visit.

"This is the nicest stadium I've ever seen," Murph said as we entered the Goal Line Bar.

Remarkably, though there were thousands of people packed around it, the Goal Line Bar wasn't rowdy. Murph and I were disappointed: we'd imagined singing and chanting, but instead it felt sanitized and harmless, with as many tourists and corporate types there as die-hard Spurs supporters.

We found our way to our seats in the South Stand section, meant to be a place where seventeen thousand of the most animated Spurs fans sit, modeled on the legendary Yellow Wall at Borussia Dortmund's Signal Iduna Park in Germany. We'd come ready to be on our feet the entire night but sat comfortably for the whole first half. There was some singing, though it wasn't remotely as loud as we were expecting.

The Spurs looked great in the first fifteen minutes, with several golden scoring chances. Burnley, a steel-toed boot of a football club, were in survival mode. After having been promoted from the second-tier Championship division to the Premier League for this season, they were already at the bottom of the table. Though losing this FA Cup match wouldn't count against them in the standings that mattered for relegation, the tournament was meaningful. Not only do teams get pride and glory for performing well but they receive increasingly large sums of money for each round they win, and the champions qualify for a place in other large competitions. Burnley hunkered down, and in classic Spurs fashion, after those first fifteen minutes in which they looked like a team on the cusp of greatness, they began to sputter.

The best action of the first half came from the lads immediately to Murph's right. The cluster of young men were angry Spurs supporters, and nothing is funnier to us than when fans of a team love their club so much they feel free to unmercifully abuse them.

"You're fucking shite!" a young man yelled toward the pitch. He wore a navy blue hoodie with the cockerel logo.

"Why did we even come?" another young man in a puffy jacket asked loudly. The entire section laughed. "I'm fecking serious, mates. Why? Why do we want to watch this? It's Friday night, for feck's sake! We should be having fun."

As Minnesota sports fans, we related to this kind of banter. Our state's four major men's sports teams own a very dubious record in recent history: we are currently in a thirty-two-year drought without a championship, the longest among American markets with all four major men's sports. (Note: Our women's sports rule. Shout-out to the Minnesota Lynx, four-time WNBA champs, and our women's collegiate and professional hockey teams.) The Spurs, like the Minnesota Vikings, are perennially on the cusp of breaking through, but some sort of freakish fuckery always ruins their chances: muffed kicks and asinine interceptions and pratfalls and unexpected blowouts and whatnot. Something always goes sideways for the Spurs, to the point that the *Men in Blazers* simply gave them the moniker of "So Spursy" to describe the sheer amount of bad luck and tomfoolery that afflicts the club.

In time, the lads turned their ire on Burnley.

"What do you think of Burnley?" Hoodie guy asked, in song.

"Shite!" Puffy Jacket yelled.

"Who do you think is shite?"

"Burnley bastards, fucks, and cunts!"

"We hate Burnley and we hate Burnley and we hate Burnley and we hate Burnley and we hate Burnley!" they began shouting in unison.

Murph was absolutely reveling in the authentic English profanity. Looking at how happy he was, I got a little emotional. I was reminded of how I felt as a young man soaking in the atmosphere at Minnesota Kicks and Strikers games. This was the sort of football fandom and action that we wanted to experience.

The action in the game dialed up when the Burnley manager, Vincent Kompany, made a substitution to put a fleet of young players with speed and skill into the game. They probed the Spurs' back line into the second half, hungry and fighting while the home team remained uninspired.

With the game knotted at 0–0 late in the contest and no one really seeming to try to win, the Burnley goalie wildly threw the ball in an attempt to start a fast break counterattack. Spurs defender Pedro Porro intercepted it.

Porro took two dribbles and decided to end the game right then and there. He unleashed a hit of dreams, a screamer from outside the box that had zero rotation and exploded into the far corner of the goal. The shot was so clean that Burnley's goalie didn't even move.

After the DARE Skywalk and the Goal Line Bar and all the rest, Murph and I had both been left with the impression that the Premier League was more flash than heart. Everything was a bit much: shiny, and new, and show-offy. I had decided the in-person experience of a Premier League game wasn't really my thing.

But at that moment when the Spurs scored to win the game, the stadium erupted with deafening applause and song, and I was reminded why I love the Premier League. For all its glamour and money, these were some of the most skilled players in the world, and they regularly produced moments of absolute wonder.

Murph and I floated out of the stadium happy, not only with the feeling of a night redeemed but also of what it represented to us. After all these years, through all the pain and the healing, we were still together, father and son, tethered together by football. It was a moment to reflect, take stock, and be grateful for this special time in our lives, the realization of a dream for two grinders like us.

Sarah would continue on with me in England for another two and a half weeks, but Murph would soon be off back to the States to start his spring semester. And for me, it was the start of something new. While the Spurs had provided me with the first steps in the journey, the next day I was heading as symbolically far away from the glitz of the Premier League as possible. My next destination was the rebel alliance of a non-league football club based in the outskirts of East London.

## CHAPTER TWO

# London Borough of Newham, East London, January 6, 2024

I was on the District Line train to the farthest reaches of East London, way out past Mile End and Bromley-by-Bow and West Ham. It had only been two days since I'd visited the Imperial Star Destroyer that is the Tottenham Hotspur Stadium. Now, I was attempting to travel as far away from the English Premier League galaxy as I possibly could without leaving the city.

As far as I could tell, there were no other tourists in my train car. It was standing room only with bone-tired shift workers, and I was squished in, shoulder to shoulder, with nurses in scrubs, cooks in their starched whites, retail and fast-food-restaurant staff wearing their mandated name tags and uniforms. They were mostly immigrants, it seemed—from Africa, and Asia, and closer by.

I hung on to the upper railing next to an Irishman. His workman's pants had built-in knee pads. His top was covered in plaster dust and his fingers were stained with gunk. He wore a *Peaky Blinders* hat that was pulled down low, hooding his eyes. He spoke sternly into a cell phone. I noticed his grotesquely mangled ear. It looked like it had been chewed on by a dog.

"It's me money, it's me wages he's after," he said into the phone.

Welcome to East London, I thought.

My destination was the Old Spotted Dog, the oldest senior football ground in London and the home pitch for a team called the Clapton Community Football Club (Clapton CFC). They played in the Eastern Counties League Division One South, tier 10. This division was quintessential non-league football, with grassroots teams that were many rungs below even the semiprofessional leagues. Regional feeder leagues like this one made up the base of the English football pyramid.

Clapton CFC was more than just a club that toiled in a level of English football I had never heard of until recently. Clapton CFC was a movement. They were a mindset. They were the change they wanted to see in English football.

They were the resistance.

Clapton CFC is explicitly supporter-owned, supporter-run, anti-fascist, anti-sexist, anti-racist, anti-homophobe, and anti-transphobe. They welcome everyone to their home matches. Specifically, they offer a safe and affordable space to enjoy the beautiful game for the most marginalized groups in English football: the working poor, the nonworking poor, people of color, immigrants, and the LGBTQ community.

I exited the District Line train at the Upton Park station. The high street was teeming with people rushing about their Saturday afternoon. There was no space or time to think. The current of foot traffic pushed me along. A cacophony of inner-city sounds engulfed me: the metallic screech of trains, the piercing hiss of bus brakes, the relentless honking from cars jockeying for position, and the annoyingly repeated cartoonish beeping from scooter horns wielded by dive-bombing squadrons of food delivery drivers.

This part of East London was a classic outer borough. It was ethnically diverse, packed tight with both white and Black Cockney East Enders as well as immigrants. It was a place where cash was king. The sidewalks snapped with the broken-bottle accents of the locals and the intermingling languages of the Middle East, Asia, Africa, and the Caribbean. The air smelled of fryer oil and spicy stew. Vendors stood near crates of produce at their storefronts, gesticulating like auctioneers to the throng of people taking a gander. There were takeout joints that sold pizza and burgers and kebabs and fried chicken and fish and chips. A fishmonger stood under fluorescent lighting in a crisp white jacket and gracefully laid fresh seafood on piles of ice. There was a store that only sold two things: fruit and fireworks.

There was no plaza or grand concourse that guided me to the Old Spotted Dog football ground as it had done at Tottenham. There were no decorative street signs with arrows pointing the way and the distance in miles to various global tourist sites. My path to the Old Spotted Dog was appropriately marked by a classic staple of the punk rock movement: stickers illegally stuck to lampposts and utility boxes. They featured cartoon characters in Clapton CFC kits, like Charlie Brown and the *Simpsons* character Groundskeeper Willie, proudly indicating the right direction for me to go.

The lampposts were also covered with stickers that got progressively more radical as I moved closer to the ground. They said "Anti-Fascism Is Community Self-Defense," and "Refugees Didn't Take Away Affordable Housing. Rich Landlords and Greedy Politicians Did" (featuring a man punting the ass of the cartoon Mr. Monopoly). They said "Eat Pasties, Punch Nazis" and "Fuck the Tories," which featured a kid flashing the backwards peace sign (an obscene gesture equivalent in England to the middle finger). One said "Your Sticker's a Cunt," beside the logo of the Football Club United of Manchester, which was formed by former supporters of the Premier League team Manchester United after they'd become disaffected from the club's gross greed and poor ownership.

This sticker was in conversation with another that was equally rebellious but far more subtle. On a red background, in the font of the famous LEGO logo, the bubbly letters CCFC were written in white and black. Beneath that it read "Build Your Own Club." This innocent-looking bit of Clapton CFC paraphernalia harkened back to the revolution that the team's supporters had sparked in East London in 2018.

The original Clapton Football Club (Clapton FC, *not* to be confused with Clapton CFC) was formed in 1878 and began playing at the Old Spotted Dog in 1887. Since their inception, they were a proper club for the hardworking Cockneys. In 1890, they became the first English club to play in Europe when they beat a Belgian team in Antwerp. They were two-time winners of the Isthmian League and five-time winners of the FA Amateur

Cup. They also had a long history of inclusivity. In 1908, Clapton FC launched the career of Walter Tull, one of England's first Black players, who went on to play for Tottenham and Rangers FC. (He also became the very first Black British army officer.)

Clapton FC members had a voice in how the club was run from the start. In fact, this right was stated in the club's constitution. But under the stewardship of Chief Executive Vince McBean, which started in 2000, supporters claimed they were shut out from decisions, including the one when McBean raised the ticket prices. It was only a few pounds, but that wasn't the point. This wasn't the English Premier League, where seeming price gouging was the accepted norm. This was a part of East London where people were used to milking every last penny from every pound. The Clapton supporters took their case to the league office, but they were met with nonaction. They kept voicing their complaints for years and years. Nothing changed.

Then in 2017, the most active group of supporters, the Clapton Ultras, decided to lead a season-long boycott of all home games. They would still watch the matches, of course—these were superfans, after all—but they'd do so by standing on discarded refrigerators and toilets and tables around the perimeter of the stadium to peer over the walls, holding arms aloft with Clapton FC scarves and singing their supporter songs.

When McBean tried to liquidate the charity that owned the lease for the Old Spotted Dog, a move that would result in a personal windfall for him, the fans hired lawyers. As the courts sorted through the bitter feud, the landlords of the Old Spotted Dog repossessed the field. It turned out McBean's organization owed them money.

The Old Spotted Dog was shuttered. With routine maintenance a thing of the past, the pitch became an apocalyptic prairie of tall grasses and weeds. Trees rooted right into the goal box. Old cars were mysteriously beached on the field. The Scaffold Stand, the section of seats from which the most ardent supporters had cheered and sung, became nothing more than a sad steel shed. In one of the several outbuildings on the property that McBean still had access to, he ran a speakeasy during the COVID lockdown.

In 2018, Clapton's community of supporters decided to do something radical. In their judgment, McBean had made a critical mistake. He had physically taken away their beloved team. He had physically taken away the club's home. But he could not kill what would never die: the soul of Clapton football. So, they formed their own club.

This merry band of punks and pranksters and anarchists and working-class folks and immigrants and gays and straights and everyone in between banded together and inaugurated a club that was for the people and by the people. They named it the Clapton Community Football Club, naturally. They even secured a spot in the same division as Clapton FC.

Clapton CFC was to be member-owned and run as a collective. Instead of power residing with an ominous board of directors, as is the case with most English football teams, it would be held by the community. The team cobbled together coaches and players from every corner of East London. While their ancestral home lay dormant, they moved their home matches around and settled at an overgrown pitch in Walthamstow that became known as the Stray Dog.

Then, in a remarkable turn of events, the leasehold for the Old Spotted Dog became available again. Clapton CFC went through litigation, raised money, and eventually secured the rights to play at their beloved home pitch in 2020. They also designed a new uniform that represented their club ethos. The red and yellow and purple design was inspired by the flag of the Second Spanish Republic, which itself had honored the International Brigades who fought in the Spanish Civil War. An anti-fascist rallying cry from the 1930s—"*no pasarán*," meaning "they shall not pass"—was written on the back of the jersey. They made more than $140,000 in one day of selling it.

An army of volunteers were enlisted to clean up the Old Spotted Dog. During the reclamation project, a Clapton supporter sprayed a message on the back wall of the Scaffold Stand:

"This Ground Belongs to You and Me."

Do not mistake Clapton CFC's sloganeering as a trite restatement of what English football already represented. Though the Premier League has peddled its own similar slogan, "Football Is for Everyone," for years, that has not been a reality for huge parts of English society.

The atmosphere in the football grounds throughout the United Kingdom, from the lower leagues all the way to the top, has often been hostile and xenophobic. Through the repeated use of racist and homophobic and sexist chants, people of color and immigrants and women and the LGBTQ community have been openly made to feel unwelcome. This was especially true during the dark period of the late 1970s and '80s, when England was the rancid beating heart of hooliganism in football.

The British economy was in a punishing recession from the early seventies to the early eighties, and it put polite British society into a free fall. There was record unemployment that sparked riots and urban strife throughout the country. Eventually the misery in the homes and on the streets was brought to the football grounds, especially in the forgotten industrial and factory towns. "Terraces," the sections of a stadium where the most hardcore supporters of a team would stand, were usually physically separated from the general public by fencing or cages. In these rowdy environments, the working class and poor found the rare place where they were seen and heard and welcomed.

It turned out that confining a bitter populace in cages suited for farm animals, however, was a terrible idea. Soon, belligerence and hooliganism and nationalism seeped in, and English football entered an era marred by fights and mayhem. Every football club had its own group of armed hooligans known as a "firm." When Millwall's players battled Luton Town's on the pitch in 1985 at Kenilworth Road, Luton's home ground, Millwall's firm, known as "the Bushwackers," fought Luton Town's firm, known as "MIGs," in the streets and in the stands. It was March 13, 1985, and as the game played out on the field, the Bushwackers laid siege to the stadium, tearing out the seats and using them as spears. The game was postponed multiple times as a hailstorm of bottles, cans, and nails were thrown on the home supporters. At the final whistle, Millwall lost 1–0 and their supporters invaded the pitch and began attacking the Luton Town players and coaching staff.

When these firms went to war, the police, viewed as a strike force for the politicians who were putting the squeeze on the working class, were all too happy to meet them with batons, dogs, shields, and fire hoses.

Due to the persistent threat of violence in the stands and the piss and pints running down the aisles, attending an English football match became a rather unsavory experience. The extent of what was plaguing the English game came to the wider world's attention after the Hillsborough Tragedy in 1989, where ninety-seven Liverpool supporters were crushed to death on the terraces of Hillsborough Stadium in Sheffield, England. An investigation ensued, and the government stepped in to clean up the sport.

But even in the 1990s and 2000s in English football, the stench of hooliganism was still present. It was not uncommon to attend football matches and see banana peels thrown at Black players, hear graphic homophobic slurs sung, and notice a hissing sound directed toward Jewish players and fan bases, meant to mimic the Nazi gas chambers. In the shadows of the bright lights shining on David Beckham's golden foot, the beautiful game could still be quite ugly for a lot of people.

The Clapton Ultras always wanted to be a different kind of firm. Instead of spouting fascist ideals and violent rhetoric, the Clapton Ultras were dedicated to the causes of radical happiness and collective joy. They hosted fundraisers and organized food banks for refugees and migrants. They supported anti-racist groups and a group called Football v Homophobia. They also got behind women's football.

Occasionally, there were retaliations. When Clapton welcomed Asian players onto the team after the 7/7/2005 Islamist terrorist attacks in London, arson was committed at the Old Spotted Dog. Another time, the Clapton Ultras and other supporters of the club were attacked by fascists during a match in Thamesmead. The violence spilled over onto the field and the game had to be canceled. Undeterred, Clapton fans dug in, and until the breaking point with McBean in 2018, they kept the good vibes, positive chants, Reggae tunes, local pies, and "no one is illegal" mantra going at the Old Spotted Dog.

No surprise, then, that when they had the chance to form their own team, they brought this ethos over.

The contrast from Tottenham Stadium couldn't have been starker as I approached the ticket booth at the Old Spotted Dog. A price of four pounds (about five dollars) was listed as the "suggested" one for tickets, because the booth operates on a "pay what you can afford" scale. Free passage is also given to the following groups or individuals: Newham residents, teenagers, seniors, students and apprentices, trade union members, the unemployed and those on low income, people with disabilities, refugees, asylum seekers, and undocumented migrants. There was no proof needed to qualify for any of these categories. They took your word for it.

"Hi'oh, here for the match today?" the kid behind the ticket window asked, putting down the book he was reading.

"Yeah, one ticket, please," I said. I handed him a fiver and told him to keep the change.

"Cheers!" he said, with gratitude.

Inside the grounds, I was greeted by a volunteer selling Clapton CFC jerseys and scarves and hats and pins on a folding table underneath a pop-up tent.

"Hullo, luv! How are you t'day?" the woman behind the table

asked. She was about sixty years old and had a smoky voice and a boozy good-time vibe.

"Great. I came from America to see the Old Spotted Dog and the match today," I said.

"Lovely," she said, stabbing a finger at me. "Good man."

She cackled throughout our small talk and could have been six gin martinis deep or sober as a judge. It was hard to tell.

"What's your name, luv?"

"Todd."

"Todd from America," she said with a sleepy wink. "In'joy yourself t'day."

I took a stroll, enjoying my freedom of movement: I had the loosey-goosey sense of being at a music festival. Behind one goal line and on one sideline of the pitch, homeowners were milling around their own backyards just feet away from the players doing their warm-ups. The only thing that separated the field from the fans was an unimposing railing that wrapped all the way around the perimeter.

In my chest, I could feel the drumming and chanting emanating from the Scaffold Stand, home of the Ultras. If Murph were here, he might have said it was like the Ewoks' party at the end of *Return of the Jedi*. Banners read "No Pride for Some of Us Without Liberation for All of Us" and the old Ultra standard "No One Is Illegal." The scents of beer and weed toasted the afternoon sky. At full volume, songs to the tune of "Hey Jude" by the Beatles and "White Lines" by Grandmaster Flash and "Just Can't Get Enough" by Depeche Mode and "Take Me Home, Country Roads" by John Denver were sung. After they'd faced the ultimate relegation by having their beloved club and ground taken away from them, this was their celebration, and it was riotous.

Along the sideline, there was a playdate happening with a group of kids and their dads. The dads had impossibly thick, perfectly shaggy hair and impossibly cool, shabby-chic attire. They huddled in this Radiohead Daycare talking and sipping craft beers. Elsewhere, near one of the corner flags, I walked past a tight circle of calloused Cockneys straight out of a Guy Ritchie movie. They smoked hand-rolled cigarettes and wore long overcoats with ties or classic fat guy tracksuits. Their dialect was impossible to comprehend.

Clapton CFC was playing Barkingside Football Club. Fred Agyemang, a Barkingside forward who led the league in scoring and had the physically imposing stature of boxer Deontay Wilder, cranked warm-up shots. Next to Agyemang was a teammate with braces and fresh pimples who looked like he needed his mom. This was non-league football at its finest.

The goal had a net, but at most stadiums there's a larger net behind that to catch stray shots and stop them from going into the stands. At the Old Spotted Dog, however, balls sprayed unimpeded. One shot came screaming right in front of me. I stabbed my left foot out and, with a volley, sent it back onto the pitch.

"Nice touch," an older man said to me.

"Thanks," I said.

The man wore a workman's jacket, a Clapton scarf, and a longshoreman's winter cap. He had an ageless English style, like Paul Weller.

"Hello, I'm Todd from America," I said.

His name was Mick (of course it was). He told me that he was an old West Ham supporter but got sick of all the hate and nonsense at the ground and started coming to Clapton CFC matches instead.

"I couldn't stand the atmosphere. It was all about the abuse rather than cheering for your team," Mick said. "Let's have a go at the ref. Let's have a go at the opposition. Let's have a go at your own players."

We kept chitchatting as we both kicked stray balls back onto the pitch. Mick asked me about my journey and where I was going next. I mentioned that a match in Brighton was on my radar.

"That was my first team," Mick said fondly. "I was raised just outside Brighton and started going to games by myself as a teenager. Just wonderful. Brighton is traditionally a gay and lesbian comfort zone."

"I heard that the Brighton fans used to have to deal with horrific homophobic chants sung at them," I said.

"And we would respond by chanting back, 'You're too ugly to be gay!'" Mick said, smiling. He looked at his watch and said, "Todd from America, I have to go volunteer. I'm on the grounds committee and working today."

During the week, Mick helped cut the grass, paint the lines, and move the goals. On match days, he walked the pitch.

"We have to look for any foxholes, fox poo, or anything that could be dangerous," Mick said. With my background in landscaping, I understood just what he meant.

During the match, I stood next to a group of thirtysomething business bros. I started chatting with a guy named Liam from Ipswich. His primary club was Ipswich FC, who were on the brink of promotion to the English Premier League. Liam and his mates were here today because they loved to balance the glitz and high stakes of league football matches with the folksy non-league matches. Plus, they share the same values as the supporters at Clapton. Liam was absolutely buzzing about being at the Old Spotted Dog and the current state of his Ipswich squad.

"The Tractor Boys playing Man City at the Etihad, can you imagine?" Liam said, offering up the nickname of his hometown club.

"There is nothing remotely close to this in American sports," I said.

"Where are you from in America?" Liam asked.

"Minnesota."

"Feck off. Seriously, mate?"

"Born and raised in the city of Minneapolis."

"I'm a huge Minnesota Vikings fan. I just bought a T. J. Hockenson jersey this morning," Liam said.

"Fuck outta here," I said.

"Look at it," Liam said, showing me a picture on his cell phone.

Liam from Ipswich proceeded to recite to me every one of my Minnesota Vikings nightmares—traumatizing moments that are branded into my sports-addled psyche.

"Gary Anderson wide left. Blair Walsh wide left. Forty-one–doughnut loss to the Giants. The Favre interception against the Saints. Losing to the Eagles the year the Super Bowl was in Minneapolis," Liam said. "Being a Minnesota Vikings fan is brutal, mate. But we love it, right?"

"Right?" I said, scrunching up my face.

At halftime, I stood next to the cranky Guy Ritchie Cockneys again just to listen to their accents. The referee and the linesmen and the players walked past us on their way to the locker rooms.

"You cheat'n cunts," one of the older Cockney men said to the referee and the two linesmen. He was a real fat bastard with the pink and fleshy face of a Sunday ham. This man no doubt had a menacing nickname on the streets like "Bullet Tooth Tony" or "Brick Top."

"Should've been a penalty called for Ton down there. Fecking cheating cunts," the Cockney man barked.

"Whoa, bruv, no need to talk like that here," a young Clapton CFC player said. "It's a beautiful day. Drink a beer. Have a good time, mate. Relax, man."

I observed this somewhat tense and unexpected situation here, of all places, wondering if it would escalate further. Then, everything cooled off. I didn't see why at first. Then I noticed the legendary Clapton player James Briggs had stepped up.

"What's this, then?" Briggs said.

That was all it took for everyone to chill the fuck out.

Briggs, a stud midfielder and East End urban legend, was the whole reason I knew about Clapton CFC in the first place. A few months prior, a short video had appeared in my YouTube feed. Two football teams were on an unremarkable pitch. There was no stadium. It looked like a public park. There was a drab municipal building in the background. A small scattering of people were in attendance, but by the way they slumped on the sideline railing, it looked like they had probably stumbled upon the match as they wandered through the park.

The referee plopped down the ball for a free kick and someone was filming it from the side of the goal. A player in purple socks and shorts and a wildly designed jersey stepped up to the ball to field the free kick. This was James Briggs.

He took a few steps back and sized up his chances. In front of him, four players in black and green made a wall. They stood like brave sentinels. They also grabbed their crotches to protect their nuts.

Briggs stepped up and launched a heavy shot on goal with his right foot. The four-man wall jumped into the air. The shot beaned the player on the far-left side, ricocheted high into the air, and arched back to Briggs. He looked skyward and waited. In that moment, he was Thor with his hammer, drawing in all the lightning.

When the ball finally fell, Briggs one-timed it out of the air with his nondominant left foot. From a standing position forty yards out, he unleashed a thunderclap into the top corner of the goal. It was one of the best things I've ever seen. The whole sequence lasted twenty beautiful seconds and had gone viral, twice, with millions of views.

Briggs had been kind enough to meet me to talk about his football career while I was in London. Being that close to him, I was taken aback by how tall and solid he was. He had the hulking physical presence of a debt collector. But he was, contrarily, extremely polite and kind.

"I was born in Clapton. I was about six when I started playing football in the park with my mates," Briggs said. "Then about seven, eight, I went to Leyton Orient. Then I played for my district. Hackney District." The way he said all this, it was clear how proud he was of where he came from.

His football career went on to read like a tour of London neighborhoods no one outside their borders has ever heard of: Brimsdown, Hoddesdon Town, St. Margaretsbury, and Wormley. And now, here he was at thirty years old and still playing for his local club. East End football was still a living presence in his life.

Briggs's long journey through the world of non-league football was a hard look into the life of a player as far away from the bright lights of the modern game as possible. Briggs doesn't get paid. He receives no benefits or bonuses. If he gets hurt, the recovery is all on him. He works a full-time job. He plays games for Clapton CFC on Saturdays and Tuesdays and has one training session on Thursdays. He also plays Sunday League ball for another local club, Hackney Borough. (Clapton is a town in the district of Hackney.)

"You have to want to be here to play. If you don't want to be here, there's no point in actually playing non-league football," Briggs said. "You got to love the game; otherwise, it's not going to love you back."

"Where do you work?" I asked.

"I'm the cash manager at a bank in the city."

"Do your coworkers at the bank know that you're the Andrea Pirlo of non-league football?"

"They don't," Briggs said, chuckling.

"They have no clue about your highlights? That you've gone viral on the internet?"

"No, mate," Briggs said, casually shrugging. "They do not."

"What is it that you love about playing for Clapton CFC?" I asked.

"It means a lot. It's a safe place for anyone," Briggs said. "So, no matter what gender you are, what race you are, whatever your religious beliefs are, you can be open and express yourself and no one's going to say anything bad to you."

It was a genuinely inspiring thing to hear. As a rising tide of fascism seeped into our lives around the world, this little football club had built a community that gives people shelter from the storm.

"When we win, I think it helps the volunteers and the fans a lot more than it does us, because they're happier. Not that we're not happy when we win. But it helps them because they've built this club up. When we win, they all win. It's a family."

Clapton CFC breezed past Barkingside FC 4–0 and were at the top of the table in tier 10. After the game, I was welcomed into the pub that sat in a long, squat building on the stadium grounds. A DJ played from a laptop in the corner. Supporters streamed freely into and out of the doorway, beer cans swishing about, like they owned the place. Because they did.

Aluminum foil trays of chicken curry and rice were passed around for a free dinner, and I was introduced to a carousel of Clapton CFC supporters. Everyone either volunteered time or donated money or served on a team committee.

A man named Ric Riscardo chatted me up. He wore a flat-brimmed hat, layered down jacket, and baggy jeans with the bottom cuffs rolled up to perfectly showcase his Nikes. Over time, he'd volunteered for a wide variety of jobs in merchandise, communications, and hospitality at the Old Spotted Dog. He'd built a deep understanding of the club and its ethos. He was currently the league representative as voted on at the annual club meeting.

Ric had gone to Charlton Athletic football games as a kid with his dad, a Black West Indian immigrant. His mom was a white Londoner. So the atmosphere wasn't always welcoming. It only dawned on Ric later why his dad always made them leave early.

"Growing up and going to matches through the eighties and nineties was toxic," Ric said. "It was difficult for my dad because I wanted to go to football, but he was aware that it probably wasn't the safest place for him to be. I couldn't see that as a kid. There were very few people who looked like us."

At one away match for Charlton Athletic that Ric attended against Brighton, he heard homophobic chants. At Chelsea, he heard the chant "there ain't no black in the Union Jack." At Tottenham, he heard monkey chants directed at Black players. In Liverpool, they threw bananas. If they ran out of bananas, they threw pineapples. The symbolism on that one was less clear. It didn't lessen how much damage they could do.

"I spent my youth playing along with male bluster at football," Ric said. "You want to fit in. But it's actually rubbish. When you get to an age of responsibility you understand this."

When he became a father and his own son, Milo, started asking him to go to football matches, he knew where to go.

"There was only one place that I was taking Milo," Ric said. "I don't want to put my son in a position where he is calling people out for their actions or the way they behave. I want Milo to enjoy going to football, and this is doable at Clapton Community. The higher they go up the pyramid, the more they will encounter opposition to what they stand for, though."

Mick, the man with ageless style who I shagged balls with before the match, was at the pub, too. He had just finished his work on the pitch. The sharp bite from the winter night was still on his rosy face.

"What gives you hope? About Clapton? About East London?" I asked him.

"The thing I'm most proud of with Clapton CFC is actually our women's team," Mick said, smiling. "You have to remember that women were banned from playing football from 1919 through 1975. Banned from any form of football, let alone playing with men. When we formed Clapton CFC, we didn't have a women's team because we had no way of recruiting young women players. Then two remarkable women named Julia Leaff and Ellie Guedalla cofounded a Clapton CFC women's team and training. Both of them had wanted to play football as youngsters but weren't allowed to. They started an open-access 5v5 using a bit of finance from Clapton CFC to help out. They gave women a safe space to play."

Julia and Ellie have now coached more than three hundred players, hosted tournaments, and fielded five-a-side teams. They lead Saturday morning sessions with women of all ages and skill levels. For their efforts, they won a London FA Award, among other accolades.

"Then our Clapton CFC women's team went on a glorious FA Cup run," Mick said as he took a pull from his beer can.

Founded in 1970, the Women's FA Cup is set up in the same way as the men's side. In 2021, the Clapton CFC women's team made history by becoming the first seventh-tier team to compete in the third round. Due to their lower non-league status, they had to play all their matches on the road. They beat Haringey Borough and Biggleswade United and Bedford and then Hounslow, a club four divisions higher. They had to travel to Plymouth, 250 miles away, and stay the night. So the supporters started a fundraiser to help pay for the trip. The prize money for reaching that level in the Women's FA Cup was still shockingly low. So Clapton CFC did what they usually did when they were confronted with injustice: They led a revolt.

"We started a campaign to increase the prize money in the lower rounds of the FA Cup," Mick explained. "A *Guardian* journalist named Suzanne Wrack got ahold of our campaign and wrote about our journey. Soon, the funding increased sixfold. All really because of us. It's gone up again this year. Still not enough compared with the men's, but at least it's something."

Mick and I stepped up to the bar for one last round. Ric was now volunteering as a bartender.

"Todd from America, what can I get'cha?" Ric asked.

I looked at the list of craft beers and cider available.

"I'll take a Thatcher's Dead cider," I said. It felt like the right choice for the vibe at Clapton.

Ric wrapped a knuckle on the bar and smiled. "Good man," he said.

## CHAPTER THREE

# Westway Sports & Fitness Centre, North Kensington, West London, January 3, 2024

Footy Addicts is a social platform that helps people to organize pickup games in the UK. Four thousand games are put together through its app each month, in more than two hundred different venues. And its mission statement speaks to me, as it's aligned with the philosophy of the Donkey Soccer League:

"Football is more than a game. It's a community, an outlet, and a way of life. Giving footy addicts a kickabout is only the beginning. Our mission is to make the nation's favorite pastime easy and inclusive. Join our community of players from all walks of life, enjoy a kickabout and make a few mates while you're at it. Our values are simple: to create a respectful atmosphere that makes football fun before anything else. Our app is available to football lovers no matter what your race, gender, or level is."

Great, I thought, when I read that on the Footy Addicts website from home as I planned my trip. Here's an approachable, low-stakes way of meeting fellow players and getting some exercise while I travel. I got in touch with the company's media manager, Jack Bies, and he was extremely helpful and supportive of both my book and my participation in pickup games. I asked where, given limited time, he might suggest I go while in the UK capital. He pointed me to the Westway Sports & Fitness Centre in West London. They were iconic, apparently—along the lines of Rucker Park for basketball players in New York—and had been used as the backdrop for loads of commercials.

That was how I found myself scratching my head beneath the graffiti-splattered underside of the A40 motorway, with Sarah's words ringing in my ears. "Please don't die," she'd said as I left our rental flat in East London to get here. What I'd taken as a joke now seemed less funny. In front of me was a row of small pitches, each one walled in with boards on the bottom and metal fencing on top. Everyone around me was half my age or younger, and juiced with an aggressive swagger like if Axe body spray took human form. I'd never been so aware of being fifty-one.

Each official Footy Addicts game has a host who welcomes the other players and sets the rules and teams. The host for my game was a man who not only resembled Biggie Smalls but ran the match in a way I imagine Biggie might have. There were no pleasantries, just orders.

"Games 'n hour. 8v8. Everyone plays goalie. Let's go, boys," Biggie said.

He casually threw out a pile of jerseys, which were devoured by the young players like a steak by a pack of piranhas. We took up positions on either side of the centerline and everyone but me immediately and aggressively started jawing at each other. Sarah's words returned to mind.

The ball was kicked into action, and I was instantly exposed as the player I truly was. In America, I may have grown up playing soccer. In the UK, I was Dorf, Tim Conway's doofus comedic character.

It was the most claustrophobic round of football I'd ever played. The intensity of the pace was constricting, each minute crushing my lungs and nervous system tighter and tighter until there was no air to breathe. The players were so skilled and so dazzling up close it made me lose my equilibrium, a seasickness on dry land. They moved the ball so quickly and processed the game so rapidly it was as if they were in a parallel reality, like the agents in *The Matrix*.

But worst of all was their anger. These young players had washed out of football academies or were spit out by the football machine or were never even given a chance in the first place, and they were still clearly pissed about it. They were taking that frustration out on each other at Westway. There was no chill here, no joy, just a lot of yelling. In a mix of accents, this ethnically diverse group of players yelled at passes made and missed. At shots made and missed. That they were open when they were open. That they were open when they weren't open. They yelled at each other. They yelled at me.

Okay, I lied. The anger was bad. But what was *truly the worst* of all was my play. This was best demonstrated by the time when Biggie asked me to guard a particular player on the other team.

"Oi, you," Biggie said, approaching me. For such a large man, he moved with terrifying speed, like a hippo in water. Then he pointed to one of our opponents. "Mark 'im," he commanded.

The player he was pointing at was twelve.

"The kid?" I asked.

"The kid," Biggie said.

It was so awkward. The kid wore a Belgium national team jersey with De Bruyne on the nameplate. His dad was standing on the other side of the fence watching his son's every move. The ball was put into play, and when I stepped up to the kid to mark him, it was like trying to guard a gnat. As soon as he got the ball, he undressed me with a series of moves on his way to score a goal. A flurry of verbal arrows rained down on me. There was nowhere to run and hide. I just stood there and took them.

"Get in goal," Biggie said to me.

I was paraded to the goal in an epic and humiliating walk of shame, Cersei Lannister–style in *Game of Thrones*. Within seconds, the piranhas on the other team started feasting. They unloaded—and I mean *unloaded*—shots on me from close range. One after another blistered right past me.

"Oi, get outta goal," Biggie said.

Without an ounce of pride left in my body, all that remained was terror. I suffer from Crohn's disease, an irritable bowel syndrome, and when I get stressed, the anxiety usually manifests itself in my lower intestines. For the last half hour of the game, the abuse and angst set upon me compounded, and a large gas bubble grew inside my body. Suddenly, I was trying to run and chase and defend the wunderkind while I had a small and solid pain firmly inserted into my anus. It was like playing footy with a butt plug in.

When the game mercifully ended, not a single player said a word to me. I left the cage and went to untie my boots at a picnic table, while trying to decide whether I'd ever made a worse decision in my life. In the 1990s, I'd once attended the famous Testicle

Festival in Missoula, Montana, and eaten deep fried cow balls, aka Rocky Mountain oysters. That was better than this.

From the picnic table, I noticed an elevated, larger field above the cages I hadn't seen before. It had stadium seating. I could hear banter and laughter.

Gingerly, I made my way over and approached the fence. There were loads of middle-aged players, many of them with joints wrapped in neoprene sleeves and braces. These were the telltale signs of wounded football vets. They had their hands on their hips from exhaustion, and even though a few looked like they might barf, they were laughing.

This was the kind of game I'd imagined being part of when I discovered Footy Addicts. In a couple of weeks, my itinerary would swing back through London. Assuming my body was recovered by then from what I'd just put it through, and my heart was recovered from the humiliation I'd just suffered, maybe I'd consider coming back to Westway.

CHAPTER FOUR

# Goodison Park, Liverpool, January 7-14, 2024

After a week in London, Sarah and I took a train north to Liverpool. Meeting us there were two of my friends from Minneapolis, Luca Gunther and John Munson. Luca, John, and I spend the wee hours of weekend mornings texting each other while we watch live English football matches from our couches. While John, like me, is a Wolverhampton supporter, Luca is devoted supporter of the club we came to Liverpool to see. And it's not the one that shares its name with the city. Liverpool FC are the new kids in town, founded in 1892. We were here to see Everton, the Old Testament of English football clubs, established in 1878. Everton—nicknamed the Toffees for reasons likely related to the candy, though the history is disputed—were a founding member of the English Football League in 1888, and the Premier League in 1992. We wanted to experience Goodison Park, the team's fabled 132-year-old stadium, before the club moved to a new stadium being built about two miles west, along the River Mersey. First we'd take a stadium tour, and a few days after that we'd go to a game.

While Sarah set off for the museums of downtown Liverpool and then the countryside, where she could take gentle walks while imagining herself to be one of the Bennet sisters from *Pride and Prejudice*, Luca, John, and I headed to the Walton neighborhood. Downtown Liverpool had a buzzy, Times Square feel. Walton was a different matter. Its main streets were clogged with discount grocery stores, the equivalent of dollar stores, fast-food restaurants, and diners. A small bodega on every block sold alcohol, snacks, and smokes. There were numerous pawnshops and gambling parlors. Even in broad daylight, there was a real sense that crime was an industrious presence here: guards stood in front of every storefront. Sneakers hung off the power lines.

There are people in the Walton neighborhood who don't even consider themselves to be English. They are Scouse, a term for a native of Liverpool. Scousers have a hardened sense of Us versus Them, an antiestablishment ethos that traces back a century to when the city was flooded with Irish immigrants due to the potato famine and was sneeringly referred to as the capital of Ireland by the plumy politicians and aristocrats in London. For decades, the people of Liverpool were suffering in the streets and had no need for a monarchy and governance by nitwits with fancy crowns upon their heads. In the modern era, during a horrific economic downturn, Margaret Thatcher and the conservative Tories neglected to provide enough resources to the city and its people, a process that was referred to as "managed decline."

After the Hillsborough Tragedy in 1989, when ninety-seven Liverpool Football supporters died, a large cover-up by the police and politicians took decades to rectify. This only solidified the sense that Liverpool was on its own. The feeling in the streets was that they were not in England but rather they were their own country. They have their own distinctive accent. They boo the national anthem. They have their own societal norms, a shifting blend of morals and rules and street justice, of what is considered acceptable and what isn't. In the 2024 Euros Football Tournament, when the England national men's football team played Spain, there were scores of Scousers cheering for Spain.

A huge majority of Everton supporters are Walton locals and either walk to the ground or take a local bus. The stadium is wedged into the neighborhood in the same manner that Wrigley Field fits into Wrigleyville. Every side street around Goodison Park is lined with small, tightly packed row houses and parked cars that make walking and driving a claustrophobic gauntlet. We walked past a store called Fight Outlet that sold boxing trunks and gloves, high-visibility construction gear, and football boots. That summed up the overall vibe of the blocks surrounding the stadium.

At Goodison Park, there's no stadium plaza like at Tottenham. You just enter from one of the narrow, busy streets. Luca and John and I found our way to the check-in area for the tour, nothing about which gave us the sense that this team was part of the world's wealthiest football league. An older man found our names on a piece of paper attached to a clipboard and scratched them out with a Bic pen. There were no scanners. No wristbands. No headsets. No computer tablets.

"Simple as you like," Luca whispered. We were charmed by the bare-bones operation, but his football heart in particular was glowing with pride for his club.

There were about fifteen of us gathered in the reception area for the tour, standing beside a small table with a framed picture of a longtime guide who had recently passed away. Lily Barnes had started working at Goodison Park in 1979 and had an encyclopedic knowledge of the stadium and the club. Her tours were apparently known for their intimate and personal touches, like visiting Grandma in her forever home. Beneath her photo was a book where people wrote their condolences.

As we started the tour, Luca struck up conversation with his fellow supporters. They were curious about how he'd ended up an Everton fan. It was a reasonable question: Americans often pick their Premier League clubs out of a mix of whimsy, ideals, persona, history, access to certain televised games, and the makeup of their friend groups. I have friends who support clubs because the team is located in the town where they studied abroad or the team has a history of supporting their specific religious faith or it is supported by their favorite musicians or they are glory hunters or they simply like the club's kit. In Luca's case, he became an Everton fan because he didn't want to jump on the bandwagon of a top-six club (Arsenal, Chelsea, Liverpool, Manchester United, Manchester City, and Tottenham). He is an avid supporter of Minnesota United, our local Major League Soccer club, which was coached from 2017 to 2023 by a former Everton player named Adrian Heath. (Luca was delighted to learn Heath, who stands around five-six, was nicknamed "Inchy" by his teammates.) Drawn by that connection to look into Everton's history, he discovered they've been perennial underdogs in the modern era and play in a relic of a stadium in front of a passionate fan base rife with gallows humor. That was enough: he was sold. He would support Everton and be a Toffee. As he told the others on our tour: "Like a horoscope, everything I heard about the club and community seemed to fit me perfectly. Plus, it's great to suffer along with the supporters. Our victories are all the tastier!" He closed his riff with a cliché, but I knew it was genuine to his experience, and it felt like the perfect thing for the moment. "I didn't find Everton, Everton found me," he said.

Our tour guide didn't wait long to list off the club's accomplishments, but once he began, we had to wait a long time for him to stop. "Everton was the first club to be presented with the League Championship trophy, the first club to present medals for winning the Championship, the first club to stage an FA Cup final—Notts County versus Bolton Wanderers, 1894—the first club on Merseyside to win the FA Cup (1906), the first club to go on an overseas football tour, the first club to construct a purpose-built football stadium, the first club to have a four-sided stadium with two-tier stands, the first club to have a stadium with a three-tier stand, the first club to issue a regular match program for home fixtures, the first club to have a player—Dixie Dean—score sixty league goals, the first club to wear numbered shirts from one to eleven (1933 FA Cup final), the first club to have a church attached to its stadium, the first club to install dugouts, the first club to install undersoil heating, the first club to win a penalty shoot-out in the European Cup (1970, versus Borussia Mönchengladbach), the first club to play four thousand top-flight games, the first club to amass five thousand league points, the first club to play one hundred seasons in the top flight, the first club to stage a World Cup semifinal in Britain, the first club to break the one-hundred-thousand-pound transfer threshold when Alan Ball moved from Blackpool for one hundred ten thousand pounds in 1966, the first club to be featured in a TV game (August 1936, versus Arsenal), the first club to have a scoreboard, the first club to have its own podcast, the first club to have its own online social networking site, and the first club to sell tickets via text message."

"Now *that* was an impressive performance," John said, leading a round of hearty applause. He knew such a thing when he saw it: John is a professional musician, best known for playing bass in the Minneapolis-founded bands Semisonic and Trip Shakespeare.

We toured team dining areas that had the feel of a place that a working-class family might rent for a wedding. We saw the visiting team locker room, which looked like the changing rooms at a public pool: wooden benches, no personal storage areas, an open shower area with just a few shower heads, known for having mysterious heating and cooling problems that only occurred on game days. Next door was the home dressing room, which was only marginally nicer: it had a few large hot tubs, a single exercise bike, and a single training table.

There was one more particularly notable moment of the tour, this one a showing of spontaneous emotion instead of a recital. In a hallway lined with portraits of all the Everton teams, I fell to the back of the group and found myself talking to a woman in her late seventies. She stopped in front of one of the pictures, and as I looked over to her, I saw her eyes had begun to well.

"This one is mine," she said softly, reaching out a shaky finger to touch the photo. "1952. It's from my first game. My father took me."

Her name was Janice, and in her childhood home, supporting Everton wasn't optional. The club was a full-fledged member of the family.

"He took me during a time when women and certainly young girls didn't go to the games," she told me of her father. "But he always took me."

When the tour eventually moved on to the pitch itself, I politely stepped up to Janice as she gazed at the stands.

"Do you remember where you sat when you first came here with your dad?" I asked.

Her right arm came up immediately and she pointed as hard and true as a compass needle. "There, first lower section along the field, in the corner, fifth row up, third seat in," she said, smiling.

Some memories don't fade.

A few days later, I was back at the stadium for Everton's match against Aston Villa. I stood outside St. Luke's, the church attached to Goodison Park, waiting for Graeme Davies, a twenty-five-year-old Evertonian who had garnered a reputation as one of the most die-hard football fans in Liverpool.

Graeme had requested that we meet at St. Luke's, as it is the home of prayers and baptisms and funerals for so many Evertonians. The ashes of the most loyal supporters are spread out in a private courtyard. Sunday mass had just gotten out. A gaggle of older churchgoers in large puffy coats stood around chatting, leaning on canes and walkers. The tips of blue Everton scarves poked out from under their coats. I found Graeme by a statue of the Holy Trinity of Evertonian footballing legends: Alan Ball, Colin Harvey, and Howard Kendall.

"Thank you for taking the time today," I said to Graeme. "I sincerely appreciate it."

"'Tis no problem at all. Happy to have you, mate," he replied. He seemed genuinely friendly, his smile and handshake were warm, but he also crackled with the intensity of game-day jitters. I knew that he might be feeling even more nervous because he was making an exception to his typical ritual to host me. Usually, Graeme arrives at Goodison Park within half an hour of game time and walks quietly to the ground alone, unpolluted by the nonsense. He avoids the pubs, the booze, the banter, the crowds, the carousing, and the club shop. "This means too much to me to get caught up in all of that other stuff," he told me. He will meet a small group of close friends for a chat and that's about it. Nonetheless, he was a gracious enough parishioner to welcome a strange traveler into his house of worship.

Graeme and I entered the church building, where he directed me up a winding staircase to the second floor. We came into a large room with light pouring in through huge windows. There was a stage at the far end. There were booths and tables lined up along the walls and in the middle of the room, stacked with clothes and books and framed photographs and souvenirs. It looked like every church rummage sale I've ever been to. Except everything in the room was a historical artifact of Everton Football Club.

On home match days, the Everton Historical Society hosts this market before the game. It's a community hub for fans to check in with each other and to be immersed in their collective history as supporters.

We looked at a booth that contained hundreds of old game programs, stacked in neat piles by the year. Men and women were scouring the pamphlets for a piece of memorabilia that connected to a memory inside them.

I randomly picked one up. It was a Watford match day program from Saturday, February 24, 2007, when Everton played at Vicarage Road. The graphics on the front looked deliciously outdated. The kits were blousey and oddly colored. I showed the program to

Graeme. He looked at it closely. His eyes moved up and down over the cover, like a scanner.

"Everton won three-nil," Graeme said confidently. "Leon Osman hit a screamer outside the box. We scored on a penalty, too. Andrew Johnson took the penalty."

I set it down and blindly picked up another program. This one was from an FA Cup Fourth Round Replay at Goodison Park on February 4, 2009.

"One-nil win over Liverpool. Those fecking rats. Steven Gerrard went off with an injury. Prick. It was zero-zero. Then Dan Gosling, nineteen years old, scored inside the box at the one-hundred-eighteenth minute. Fecking beauty."

I stared at Graeme, stunned. This was *Rain Man*–type shit.

"What?" he asked, shrugging.

Graeme worked the room, smiling and chatting up the vendors. His jitters seemed to have gone. He seemed to feel at home, walking with the intimacy and familiarity of a man at a family reunion. Here, he was among the people who shared his angst caused by Everton's current position at the bottom of the table. Here, he was among people who shared memories of better times.

"Big match today, isn't it," Graeme told me. "Everton's under siege at the moment. It's us against the wald."

In their long and illustrious history, Everton have played more games in the top division of English football than anyone else, winning nine league titles, one European Cup, and five FA Cups. They've only been relegated twice in all of their 132 years:

1929–30 and 1950–51. They'd remained in the Premier League since its founding.

But for three consecutive years now, they'd been flirting with breaking that streak. This season was the most dangerous of all. In October 2023, Everton's long-serving chairman Bill Kenwright died of cancer, leaving the club adrift. This was particularly bad timing, as the team was under investigation for alleged financial misdealing, overspending in a way that other clubs claimed had helped them stay out of relegation. The next month, in November, they were handed down a brutal punishment: a deduction of ten points in the league table. Teams get three points for each match win, one point for a draw, and no points for a loss. The absolute best teams usually finish the season with points totals in the eighties and nineties; the worst—those in and around the relegation zone—in the twenties and thirties.

To the embattled supporters, the whole thing stank of English football jobbery. They were certain the points deduction was proof that the forces in power wanted to kick Everton out of the Premier League. This was bolstered by their questions about why Manchester City, which was also accused of violating financial rules, hadn't yet suffered any points deductions. (City strongly denied any wrongdoing and explained they had irrefutable evidence that would clear their name.) An organization called the 1878s had been leading protests against the EPL brass at recent Everton home matches, making their home in the most famous section of Goodison Park's stands, the Gwladys End. I had tried repeatedly to contact the 1878s but hadn't gotten a response. As an unsanctioned group not officially connected to Everton Football Club, the 1878s preferred to work in the shadows.

Even before 2023, Everton had been in trouble. "Everything at the club over the last two seasons has been a complete mess," Graeme said, referring to 2021 and 2022. They'd spent those years barely escaping relegation with a blend of anxiety-riddled last-minute heroics, black magic, and divine intervention. This had strained the relationship between the club and supporters like Graeme, who felt the players were lacking in effort and not identifying with the same values of the fans.

"But now we are seeing an Everton team with players that have team spirit, willing to run through brick walls for us as fans," Graeme was proud to report. "They are fighting for every single ball. Every tackle is there. They are all backing each other up. Honestly, half the battle is won because of the players by their work ethic and work rate alone. We have to be up for it from the start."

Everton's current roster could not win on talent alone. They had to put in hard work, show grit, and hope for a little luck, just like how most people got by in Walton. The team didn't possess a single superstar who could unlock a game all by himself. They needed all the help they could get. Luckily, the players weren't alone. Graeme believed that the Everton players and Everton supporters were a united front.

"At the minute, the team and the fans are completely one. The unity there is something I haven't seen in a long time. Not since David Moyes was the manager," Graeme said. "We are now seeing an Everton team that can identify with the fans. They play the way fans expect, with the desire we expect."

To make the pain of the past few seasons sting just a bit more, Everton's recent relegation battles had coincided with the breathtaking ascent of their bitter rivals right next door. Liverpool FC plays less than a mile away from Goodison Park, at a stadium called Anfield. However, Everton supporters do not recognize or answer to the typically used term "Liverpudlians" because it has the word Liverpool in it. That's how much they hate the Reds. Luca, John, and I had gotten a taste of this after our tour of Goodison Park, when we'd casually walked over to Anfield. John and Luca were wearing blue Everton winter hats. A cabdriver spotted us and screamed out of his window. "Oi, you two! In the Everton caps! Get into the cab NOW!" We hesitated, unsure of what he was up to. "TOFFEES GET IN NOW," he shouted.

It turned out he was a die-hard Everton supporter and was trying to protect us. There was a huge sticker on his fiberglass partition that said: "GOODISON GANG." "Oi, you lads, if you're Everton supporters, you have to now burn your fecking shoes for being on that unholy ground," he told us. "I'm fecking serious." Graeme later confirmed this: "When we go to Anfield, we all buy shoes at one of the charity shops before the game. After the game, we throw them away. Our feet and our own shoes never touch that shite hole."

Over the last five years, Liverpool FC has demonstrated a sizzling, sexy style of play, the very embodiment of the beautiful game. In the 2018–2019 season, they won the Premier League, and in the 2019–2020 season, they won the Champions League. While Everton's roster has been full of mudders and plow horses, Liverpool has been home to a stable of thoroughbreds, world-class players from around the globe whom their analytics department has successfully scouted, recruited, and acquired.

Meanwhile, with construction underway on Everton's new stadium across town, the club's supporters were worried about losing touch with tradition. Goodison Park will not be torn down, though. It will become the permanent home to the Everton Women's Football Club. The team and its wealthy foreign owners were trading the grand old lady of Goodison Park in for a hot young trophy wife in a soon-to-be hip and gentrified neighborhood. Every day, new barbs about the shiny thing being built for a team currently in the relegation zone landed against the Toffees. The running joke was that Everton was building a billion-dollar Championship division stadium. Worse still, Michael Jones, a lifelong Everton fan working construction on the new stadium, had died during a horrific accident, casting a pall over the whole project.

Graeme feels all this acutely. The fate and glory of Everton and his well-being are two strands entwined inside him, a double helix of football and life. Graeme was two years old when he came to his first match at Goodison Park. He now attends every single Everton match that they play in the English Premier League, thirty-eight per season, plus most other matches they play, whether for exhibitions or tournaments. He has traveled to see them in Singapore, the Netherlands, Germany, France, Austria, Switzerland, Ukraine, Russia, Cyprus, Slovakia, Italy, Belgium, Croatia, Portugal, and Saint Paul, Minnesota—where he happened to be sitting behind my brother. That's how I'd gotten connected to Graeme: they'd struck up a conversation after Graeme let fly a flurry of expletives at the lack of effort the Everton players had shown in the loss, and he apologized to Tony and my nieces Adeline and Olivia. They exchanged numbers.

"Liverpool is a city full of poverty. But we just really care about football. It's what we look forward to. It is the one thing that gets us through the week," Graeme told me. "I remember we brought four thousand supporters to London on a Thursday night, just after Christmas, when everyone's low on money. I know fans, and myself included, who have not eaten in order to save money so that they can afford to buy tickets. I remember a few years ago, I didn't buy food for weeks in order to save some money to pay for a match. That's what it means to us as Evertonians; no matter how rich or poor a person is, we want to support the club we love."

On a professional level, Graeme's place of employment is understanding of his obsession. This is because he works for Everton, in their community outreach program, as a primary school tutor and sports coach. On a personal level, on his first date with his fiancée he asked her if she supported Everton or that other club in Liverpool. He simply could never date a Red.

"I could never be in a relationship with someone that supports a football club filled with rats and tourists," Graeme said.

We left St. Luke's and stood out on the sidewalk among all the game-day rabble. Graeme looked back at the church and then at Goodison Park looming over it.

"I would literally not be here without Everton Football Club," Graeme said, as a policeman on horseback clopped by. "My parents met on an Everton supporter bus going to an away match. They began dating soon afterwards. All of this is inside me. It's ingrained in me. It's in my DNA."

The literalness of this statement was about to be driven home for me. "PROGRAMS!" a tough-looking old sod bellowed from a folding table outside the church. He had a ruddy, weathered face with a bulldog's lower jaw. "Get your PROGRAMS HERE!"

"That's my dad," Graeme said. "He's a part of the Everton Football Club Heritage Society. He's selling programs today. I told you this was in my DNA."

All we could do was laugh.

It was finally game time.

To get into the stadium proper I followed Graeme through a turnstile that looked like a relic from the *Titanic.* Heavy steel, thick bars, and a grinding mechanism with huge gears. I squeezed through the gate, scanned my ticket into a reader, and forcefully moved the bar. I was inside Goodison Park.

I stepped into a dingy concrete-and-tile bathroom. There were no urinals. No troughs. Just a gutter along the wall that you pissed into. My God. The simplicity of it all.

When I rejoined Graeme, we walked up a small staircase, and then the pitch was right in front of us. Nothing can prepare you for how vivid a Premier League football pitch can look. It was so overwhelming to the senses that it elicited the sound of a symphony in my neural pathways. My eyes were soaked with a shade of green that I had never seen outside of Ireland.

We walked to the very end of the Gwladys End Stand. My seat was technically in another section, but Graeme said I could just squeeze into his row. Once there, I realized I was only a section away from where Janice, the woman I'd met on the stadium tour, had sat with her dear old dad so long ago.

Everton flags were swirling as the starting lineups walked out to a snappy drumroll that was like the sound of soldiers walking out to battle. Then came whistles and flutes and cymbals as the players formed a line on the pitch.

Someone rushed into our row and handed Graeme a plastic bag. As the live TV cameras focused on the Gwladys End, a massive item was discreetly taken out of the bag in Graeme's hands. It was folded neatly into a square.

"You're the man to hold the corner," said a stranger next to me.

I bent at the knees to brace myself as a weighty banner unfolded across the stand like a glorious sail. Supporters tugged and yanked at it as it was spread out and eventually covered almost the entire section. On the face of the banner was the Premier League lion logo with the words "EPL CORRUPT." I had found the 1878s after all!

Several other banners of similar natures were soon unleashed, rippling across the Gwladys End. A chant broke out at the top of the section, and it was like a wall of sound bearing down on me. The corner of the banner that I was holding shot up from a gust of wind and I held on with everything I had. Then suddenly the corner of the protest banner was thrust out of all our hands, sucked away from us like a fast-retreating tide. Just as the ball was kicked into play, the banner was swallowed into the sea of supporters and secreted quietly out of sight.

"Look around; notice how everyone is watching the match," Graeme said, with the match now underway.

I had a perfect view of almost the entire lower stadium. All around the bowl, I saw how the supporters talked to their neighbors but never took their eyes off the pitch, like you do when you're driving and talking to a fellow passenger in the car while keeping your eyes on the road. The scene reminded me of those old-timey photos of spectators watching baseball in the 1940s—thousands of men in hats all looking in the same direction.

And yet, the whole scene was so un-American. There was nothing to focus on but the game. There were no distractions. There was no jumbotron. There were no replays. There were no time-outs. There was no in-game music. There were no cheerleaders. There were no dancers. There were no mascots. There were no T-shirt cannons. There were no in-game concessions.

There were no in-game quizzes. There were no in-game interviews. Instead, everyone simply watched the game. Every pass, every connection, every tackle, every run, every save—all of it was given a respectful round of applause. I was shocked when something as minute as a simple slip pass between two defenders was applauded.

As Aston Villa's link-up play began to build, I could feel the engine to their fast-paced offense beginning to rev. They opened the throttle and passed forward with serious intent. The Villa wingers made probing runs. Stud forward Ollie Watkins was fast and furious and ran directly at the Everton back line and tested the goalkeeper, Jordan Pickford. Goodison Park had grown nervous and quiet. A few chants were called out but quickly whimpered away.

"We are a reactionary crowd. What we need now is a good tackle, a link-up play, a chance on goal. Something to fire up the crowd," Graeme said.

Minutes later, Goodison Park got what it needed. Everton forward Dominic Calvert-Lewin broke in alone on goalie Emiliano Martinez. Martinez had been a hero for Argentina in the last World Cup when he made the ultimate golden save to seal his team's victory. Today, he charged forward and closed down the space between him and Calvert-Lewin. He made himself big, spreading out his arms and splitting his legs. Calvert-Lewin put the shot right into Martinez's outstretched right leg. Goodison Park let out a massive groan of disappointment. But it was immediately followed by a classic Goodison Roar. The entire stadium instantly came to life and surged with energy, as if hit with the fever of evangelicals. I could feel the wall of applause in my chest.

"There it is," Graeme said.

Halftime came and the game was knotted at 0–0. Very few supporters got up to go to the bathroom or grab concessions. Almost everyone just waited in their pew for the game to start up again. They all seemed either hyper-focused in conversation about the first-half game tactics or were on their phone poring over the first-half stats and replays.

The second half began, and everyone simply stood back up. The parishioners in the Gwladys End began to cheer and yell and love and loathe in rolling swells of emotion. Faith was questioned. Faith was abandoned. The Everton supporters began to bitch at their own players. The united front between the team and the supporters that Graeme had been feeling earlier began to fray. Supporters wondered aloud why they even kept coming here. They groused about Everton manager Sean Dyche's tactics. They complained about VAR, a problematic replay system. Seconds later, they shouted their love for VAR for a decision that went Everton's way. It was all quite mental. It was all quite wonderful.

They gave their two cents to the Villa players, too. Holy hell did they give it to the Villa players. My dad worked for the Philadelphia Flyers hockey team in the 1990s and I went to countless games there. It was wild. But Philly was kindergarten cursing compared to this. The worst words and phrases I've ever heard were detonated in the open air all over the Gwladys End. When Villa made a beautiful series of passes that resulted in a quality shot on frame, the players were soundly told to fuck off by at least a thousand supporters. John McGinn, a scrappy Scottish player for Villa, was screamed at for being a "fat little shithouse." Everton's play then rebounded, and the love came back, and the applause came back, and Goodison Park roared with urgency.

At that moment, I looked around at this old place, this grand old lady, and thought about how much Everton and its supporters were losing by leaving it. It would be the equivalent of the Boston Red Sox leaving Fenway Park. What the new era for the club will look like, I don't know. What I do know is that it won't feel like Goodison Park. No matter how cool and luxurious the amenities will be, there will not be a church on the grounds that doubles as a community center for a part of the city that desperately needs it. No matter how loud the new stadium will get, no matter how the architects try to replicate the Gwladys End with a modern design, it will never sound like this. The Goodison Roar will live here forever, under these low metal roofs, vibrating off the ancient steel trusses, thundering out of the stands toward the pitch, a landslide of applause so loud it has the weight of history behind it.

Graeme began to stir. He reared up behind me. He gripped my shoulder and then stepped up on a railing next to us, lifting himself above the crowd, as if he'd stepped into a pulpit.

"Everrrr-ton! Everrrr-ton!" he began chanting, pumping a clenched fist in the air. Soon, a chorus of the Everton faithful joined him, and the chant rained down onto the pitch.

"Everrrr-ton! Everrrr-ton!"

Survival was all that mattered. When the game ended, it was nil–nil. It wasn't what they wanted, but it could have been worse. That was one more point to add to their tally. With Graeme and the rest behind them, they'd fight until the end.

This was Everton Football Club, and it was do or die.

CHAPTER FIVE

# Wrexham, Clwyd County, Wales, January 13, 2024

On a cold and drizzly Saturday morning falling between our Goodison Park tour and the game against Aston Villa, Luca, John, and I made a pilgrimage of sorts to north Wales. We were taking a leave from Everton's ancient cathedral to visit a club with the glittery fervor of a televangelist.

The Wrexham Association Football Club had seemingly crawled out from under the Bryn-y-hafod Mountains and been brought to the American public's attention through our true national pastime: staring at a screen. *Welcome to Wrexham*, the docuseries that has aired on FX and Hulu since 2022, is famously about the club owned by Hollywood actors Ryan Reynolds and Rob McElhenney. The show has been a hit with audiences and critics alike.

Wrexham AFC was founded in 1864 and is the third-oldest professional football team in the world. For most of their history they were a non-league team, but in April 2023, at the end of the second season of the show, they earned promotion out of the National League into League Two. Talk about a made-for-TV moment. Their promotion revitalized the team, the town, and the entire region in what has been called "the Rob and Ryan Effect." Tourism has increased by more than 50 percent since 2018, boutique hotels have sprung up, and businesses are now investing in and relocating to Wrexham, creating jobs and civic pride. The club has propelled what was once a tired and old agriculture and mining town in a cold and wet part of the UK into a hot spot.

When Luca and John and I set out for Wrexham, the team was playing so well it looked like they'd soon get promoted again, to League One. We arrived after an easy hour-and-a-half train ride from Liverpool to a station platform that at noon was already buzzing, three hours before game time. "Wreeeeex-haaaaammmm," people chanted, as children wearing the team's kits and colors stared wide-eyed.

The town of Wrexham had a classic high street of shops and restaurants. There was an intricate arched brick doorway over the entrance to the general market built in 1879. A gorgeous *Toiledau Cyhoeddus* (public toilet) had ornate stained glass above the entrance.

We made our way to the stadium to have a look. The journey from the reality show into the literal reality in front of me was trippy. It was as if we were walking through a montage from the show. The smell of grilled onions from the burger truck I had seen in background shots was intoxicating in real life; the sizzling grill sounded like sparklers on the Fourth of July.

We popped into the pub where the original members of the club met in 1864 to form the team. The Turf is the oldest pub at any sports stadium in the world and has been a meeting place for Wrexham fans for 160 years. It has also become a focal point for the television show. With still more than two hours to match time, the place was absolutely packed. The front room was full of men and women who were clearly longtime supporters from well before Hollywood and the television cameras arrived. The back room had a large cluster of Americans and tourists from various other places. We settled in among them, with John quickly becoming the life of the party.

I spied a man on the smoker's patio through the glass doors in the back. He had a huge salt-and-pepper beard and the look of someone with a story to tell. He also had serious Unabomber vibes. I summoned some courage and went out to introduce myself.

"Hello, I'm Todd from America," I said.

"I'm David. Or Dafydd," he replied, eyeing me up.

Dafydd squinted one eye. A cigarette dangled off his lower lip. His face was heavily weathered, deeply wrinkled around his eyes, and his nose and cheeks were nicked with scars. He wore a beat-up canvas work jacket. He looked so at home on the patio that I wondered for a moment if he *lived* out here. When he took the cigarette out of his mouth, he did not politely turn his head: the smoke emerged toward me in a plume like exhaust from a backfiring vehicle.

"Um, like I said, I'm Todd from America, and I'm traveling throughout the UK watching football," I stammered.

"Right. We have a raft of Yanks watching the game now. It's great to see, mate."

That was a relief. I loosened up. "If you don't mind me asking, how long have you supported Wrexham?" I asked.

"My whole life. I can see the lights of the stadium from my house," Dafydd said, pointing toward rolling mountains cloaked with misty clouds.

"How do you feel about the new owners?" I asked.

"Love 'em, just brilliant," Dafydd said. He took a pull from his beer, and he downright glowed with pride at the influx of money and spirit that they've brought to this tiny corner of the UK. "We were going to . . . garrr . . . ," Dafydd mumbled, like a pirate. "I don't know what was going to happen to us. They saved us. That's for sure."

When I told him about my journey, including that I had already spent time in East London, he seemed impressed.

"You are serious." Dafydd smiled. "If you were with those Cockneys, you were in some serious shite."

Just before he stubbed out his cigarette and took his leave, he showed me two pins on his jacket. The first had a shield on it.

"This is for the Welsh, my countrymen, when we fought off those Saxon bastards that tried to take our lands," he said.

The second had a club held in a clenched fist. "And this is for my old firm," he said. He looked me straight in the eye. Then he winked and left.

I stood stunned on the smoker's patio. By approaching Dafydd and chatting with him, I had unexpectedly touched the electric third rail of English football history. The dangerous and dark world of hooliganism was a subject that I studied in preparation for the trip, primarily by reading the seminal book *Among the Thugs* by Bill Buford. It is a staggeringly violent inside look into hooliganism in the 1980s in the UK. I was advised by the friends from Manchester and Ireland who are my teammates at Donkey Soccer to not bring up or ask questions about hooliganism. An American journalist nosing around in the underworld of English football would certainly not be welcome.

Even though the football firms that blighted the landscape of English football were now largely dormant, their members were still out there, seemingly ready to take up arms again at a moment's notice, ready to defend their turf and club. To literally be with one of the thugs was scary and cool and left me speechless for the first time in my life.

In the UK, even the time that a football game starts is historically significant.

The 3:00 p.m. Saturday kickoff time for the game we were about to see between Wrexham and AFC Wimbledon is a tradition dating back to when the sport was invented. As Alexander Jackson, curator at the National Football Museum in Manchester, had explained to me, it dates back to the Factory Act of 1860—a bill that decreed work must stop at 2:00 p.m. on Saturdays. This made 3:00 an ideal time for what soon became an integral leisure activity for the working class. The men played, the women and children watched, and the consistent scheduling made the game a weekly ritual.

According to Jackson, newspapers fit themselves around the new tradition, too, going to print shortly after the matches ended and reporting scores from all across the country. Jackson said they tried to be "so quick that fans could sometimes buy them on the way home from the match." Later, special radio and TV shows were created that were solely dedicated to football, and families would make a habit of tuning in every Saturday just before dinnertime. "This would reinforce [football fandom] for later generations who may not have gone to games but who would follow via the BBC," Jackson said.

In 1960, amid the huge rise in television viewing, traditionalists became worried that local clubs would lose their supporters: everyone could just go watch the top-flight games from home and stop going to their town's stadium. In response, a national rule was instituted. No 3:00 p.m. football matches could be televised live. If people wanted to watch the earlier and later games at home or from the pub, they could do so, but three o'clock was a sanctified time. To see those games, you'd have to buy a ticket and go support your team in person. As a result, very few Premier League games take place then, though there's been recent debate about whether the rule makes sense in a modern context, and arguments that it should be abolished.

For now, though, it remains in place, steeped in memory and nostalgia. It's a refuge from the mundane churn of family and work and politics. It's a rhythmic, ordered focus of ritual. It's a time for the old to feel young again, and for the young to join the tribe. It's a time to celebrate, to rear back and sing to the heavens, to feel alive. That's what I felt I was getting to be part of as I entered STōK Cae Ras, the world's oldest international football stadium. Luca, John, and I had three single seats scattered throughout the stadium, so we parted ways. My seat was right behind the goal, in a section without a roof, and even though I had on four layers, I realized that I had underdressed for a stationary afternoon in the raw Welsh winter. The sky was bruised with varying shades of blue. At the opposite end of the pitch from where I stood, there was a long row of tall trees that were flanked by two towers of floodlights that glowed in the sky like two celestial beings. Behind them were the cloud-covered mountains where Dafydd lived. A light mist began to fall.

Next to me on one side was a grandfather and his grandson. The grandpa was busy pointing to different things of note in the stadium while the child was busy with his treats. On the other side were four men in their seventies, old friends chatting breezily as they sipped hot tea and coffee. Across the field from us was the STōK Cold Brew Coffee stand, a two-tiered bunker of the most rowdy and vocal Wrexham supporters. They were tuned up and chanting. Wedged into the corner of the home stand immediately adjacent to the STōK Cold Brew stand were the AFC Wimbledon away supporters. The game was close to starting and the opposing groups were getting after each other, lobbing chants and songs that exploded like the volleys of cannon fire between two tall ships.

"You sold your soul to Mickey Mouse! You sold your soul to Mickey Mouse!" the AFC Wimbledon supporters chanted over and over, taking a dig at Wrexham's Hollywood ownership.

"WREX-UM! WREX-UM!" the Wrexham supporters fired back, drowning them out.

In the first half, I witnessed how beautiful this game can be even when goals aren't scored. There were improvised passes, free-flowing movement, galloping and heart-pounding runs up the wing, a perfectly weighted through ball that was absolutely inch perfect, a cross that skimmed the wet turf like a stone across a calm pond, and a shot on goal that had the conviction of Gabriel's horn.

I chatted with my seat neighbors and learned about the various regions and small towns in Wales and the north of England from where they hailed. Any borders between us were broken down by the universal language of football. I know it was a small moment given all that we're up against in the US and beyond, but at a time when so many people around the world are being systematically divided, I found the experience pretty healing. As I looked skyward, mist gently spritzed my face, cleansing and refreshing me. I'd gotten to know this team on television, but here I was in person, talking to other people, a part of something real. By the time the game ended, with Wrexham victorious 2–0, I felt like a man reborn.

CHAPTER SIX

# Bath, Somerset, and Bristol, January 14–21, 2024

All I want is *one day* with you on this trip, free of English football," Sarah said. "You can do that, right?"

"Yes," I said. "Yes. I can do that."

We were in Bath, walking toward the Jane Austen Centre. Sarah was a huge fan of Austen's books and the films that had been adapted from them.

"Thank you, Todd," Sarah said, squeezing my hand.

Sarah grew up in a household where sports were not played or discussed. Art was the currency, the subject of conversation, the thing to be supported. Her childhood was spent in Minneapolis's Uptown neighborhood, the Twin Cities' center of alternative culture. Her first concert was David Bowie—when she was fourteen. After she'd seen Ziggy Stardust, there was no way Twins first baseman Kent Hrbek was going to do anything for her.

But then Sarah married me, the imbecile sportswriter who had grown up gleefully eating nuclear-orange nacho cheese and chips out of plastic helmets. We'd both compromised over the years, and our relationship had been better for it. But on this trip—which we'd been on for close to three weeks—I'd given her very little of my time. And in just a few short days, she would fly home while I continued the trip alone. Sarah had been understanding over the past weeks—she knew what my purpose was and she supported it—but I could give her one day of my time. She deserved at least as much as that.

"Just for today, please don't chat up everyone you meet about football. No banter with the locals. No small talk with the barista or grocery clerk or waiter or anyone you meet on the street."

"I will behave, promise," I reiterated.

The Jane Austen Centre was in a Georgian townhouse built in 1735. Austen had not only lived in Bath in the early 1800s but set many famous scenes in her books in the city. The Centre, though not a home she'd actually lived in, was designed to be a combination of traditional museum and experiential tour—complete with character actors—to give visitors a sense of life in the Regency period.

Mr. Wickham, the villain of *Pride and Prejudice*, got us started on our tour with an oral history of Jane Austen's family tree. "The marriage of George Austen and Cassandra Leigh began at St. Swithin's here in Bath," Mr. Wickham said in a crisp, elegant accent. Wickham wore a crop-topped blue peacoat over a billowy, ruffled shirt and white pants tucked into tall boots. The actor was handsome, but every time he gesticulated, his flowy shirt cuffs flapped in a way that looked ridiculous to me, like white doves were trying to escape from under his jacket. Since the expression on Sarah's face was pure rapture, I kept the observation to myself.

Wickham soon moved on from Austen's real-life family to her literary one, recounting famous scenes from her novels that took place in Bath. "In *Northanger Abbey*, Catherine Morland runs from Milsom Street through the city to the Royal Crescent," he said, referring to a gorgeous, historic row of buildings just a few blocks away that we'd stopped to look at on our way here. Wickham noted that the Royal Crescent was also where they'd filmed the scene "where Anne Elliot is reunited with Captain Wentworth" in the 2022 Netflix adaptation of *Persuasion*. Which Sarah had watched, of course.

I did my best to put away my pretensions, and slowly, I got into the experience. Sarah and I got time to walk around the museum and read the displays without the guidance of an actor, and I really enjoyed learning more about Austen and her novels.

At the end of the museum route, we entered a sort of Jane Austen fun zone, where we could write with a quill and try on Regency period clothes and hats. I snapped photos of Sarah in her bonnet with a Mr. Darcy mannequin. Her smile was radiant. This was her everything.

Then a character actor we hadn't seen before entered the room. He was dressed in British naval attire: a navy peacoat with gold buttons, a triangle hat, white pants, and tall white socks. By now, I knew who this was, and like a kid meeting his favorite characters at Disney World, I was actually excited to see him.

"Good afternoon, sir and my lady. I am Captain Wentworth," the young man said with full panache. He tipped off his hat and bowed slightly.

"Good afternoon," I said.

"Hello!" Sarah said, gushing, still in her bonnet with her arm wrapped around Mr. Darcy.

"I see that you have met our Mr. Darcy," said Captain Wentworth as he stepped closer to us. "He is a man of good standing, indeed."

"This place is really great," I told him, meaning it.

Captain Wentworth's expression suddenly changed. He was staring at me intensely. Was there something on my face? "Clapton CFC!" he yelled in a new voice, breaking out of character.

I reached up to touch my head, remembering the hat I was wearing: a black stocking cap with the team logo on it. This wasn't good.

"I lived in Clapton!" the actor who was no longer Wentworth continued. "Have you been to a match at the Old Spotted Dog? Oh! Please tell me you've been to the Old Spotted Dog!"

My face was reddening. I remained staunchly mute. Sarah was studying me closely, waiting to see what I would do.

The actor wasn't giving up. "I'm a supporter! What are the odds of this happening?" He stuck out his hand for us to shake. I kept my hands at my side, paralyzed into this awkward position by fear. It didn't slow him down. "This is wild, mate. I've never seen a Clapton CFC hat outside the East End. Tell me how and why do you have it on?"

I leaned toward him and whispered: "Dude, I can't talk about Clapton right now. Trust me, I'd love to. But I just can't. Not today."

"God damn it!" Sarah huffed, though with a comic softness that told me she wasn't really that mad. "I can't have one day . . . ONE DAY . . . without English football!" She threw up her arms in Austen-appropriate dramatic protest. The actor, not knowing her as well, looked alarmed. "Just go ahead and tell him," Sarah said in fake disgust. "Just get it over with."

Relieved, I let it all fly. Everything I'd been holding in that day came out in a gush. "I'm Todd from America and I'm writing a travel memoir about relegation and promotion and all the levels of English football and right now I'm in the middle of a long trip through the UK and going to football matches and experiencing the culture and I've been to Spurs and Everton and Wrexham and I went to see Clapton play at the Old Spotted Dog and I loved it there and I met James Briggs the Clapton legend and he's just the absolute best guy and now I've said too much and thank you."

The actor tipped up his hat. "You're a writer! Mate! This is unbelievable. So am I! I'm working on a book of my own! And I'm a lifelong supporter of Plymouth Argyle." He started belting out Plymouth Argyle chants. In his sailor costume he was saying something about how Southampton football supporters are fish fuckers.

I realized I'd gone as far as I could. If I opened my mouth and got into it any more, Sarah's one day without English football would officially crash and burn. Somehow, thank God, the actor finally read my cues. Suddenly, he was back in character.

"My lady, I apologize for bringing up a subject that has clearly soured your mood," the actor who was now Wentworth again said. He removed his hat and bowed. "Please accept my deepest apologies."

"It's okay," Sarah said, giggling. "My husband can't help it. He is the Pied Piper of English football."

"If it pleases my lady, I will exit our current predicament and will be in the gift shop for the next fifteen minutes. If it pleases my lady, your Pied Piper may talk about such matters at his leisure in that space."

Sarah made a frown but was secretly loving the absurdity of the entire situation.

"Go on," Sarah said to me. "I'll stay here with Mr. Darcy."

Bath was just a quick day trip for us from the place where we'd gone directly after saying goodbye to Luca and John in Liverpool, and where we returned after leaving the Jane Austen Centre. It was a city with the opposite dynamic from Bath: somewhere I thought would be all about football, but turned out to not be that at all. Maybe that's why Sarah had been liking it so much.

Bristol, a port city in the southwest corner of England, is home to two football teams—Bristol City in the Championship division and Bristol Rovers in League Two. On January 15, just after we arrived, Bristol City beat the Premier League team West Ham in the third round of the FA Cup. It was a huge upset, their most important victory in the tournament since winning against Liverpool in 2014.

Then, the day after our trip to Bath, on January 20, I headed to their stadium, Ashton Gate, to see them play Watford, another Championship team. Since Bristol City had been largely irrelevant for the last decade, finishing mid-table, I expected to encounter a fan base jolted with energy from their big FA Cup performance. If they kept playing like that, they could get promoted to the Premier League! At the same time, the Bristol Rovers were playing a home game on the other end of the city.

To put it simply: I felt no buzz. Until I made it to the neighborhoods immediately adjacent to Ashton Gate, I would have had no clue that it was game day. I didn't see a single flag or banner. Come to think of it, in the days I'd spent in Bristol, I hadn't seen a mural or advertisement or store or designated pub or merchandise stand or local lad in either Bristol City or Bristol Rovers swag. Not once.

On this game day Saturday, it seemed the people of Bristol were largely just going about their lives without thinking of football. People were out walking their dogs or going for a cycle. They were enjoying the food trucks and restaurant boats along the river with their strings of party lights.

Even when I got a block from the stadium, there were no barricades. No police horses. There was no singing or carousing on the sidewalk or in the streets. I even came across a young man walking home from the park, casually dribbling a football down the middle of the street. That's how much room there was.

I found my seat in the stadium and struck up a conversation with the lads next to me. Two of the three knew fuck-all about football. The game action was meh. Instead of looking shot through with life, Bristol City seemed hungover from their big win versus West Ham.

At halftime, I went to a lounge my ticket gave me access to, where I was served hot tea and a hot pie. When I saw the teams coming out for the second half, I rushed back to my seat because, you know, I was at a football match. No one else in the lounge budged. And when I got back to my seat, no one else from my aisle was there. They never returned.

As I walked out of the stadium, a man with a Bristol City scarf said flatly, "That was a perfect stadium for a perfectly boring one-to-one draw," and, holy shit, was that spot-on.

So, Bristol wasn't a football town, at least not from what I saw. Though I was disappointed at first, Sarah had been telling me how much she loved the place on her own wanderings, how she'd found neighborhoods so cute that they made her want to move there. Even if it couldn't offer the glory and passion of football that I had come in search of, perhaps it had other charms to become acquainted with.

Sarah took me on a stroll through her favorite neighborhood, Clifton Village, a posh, leafy little hamlet. It had Georgian town houses and crescent-shaped buildings à la Bath and boutiques and independent shops and immaculately cared-for green spaces. There was a fresh flower market and a small grocer that displayed its produce in little antique wood boxes. We sat near a large front window at the East Village Café and drank coffee and ate baked goods. It was enough to make me start entertaining the idea of moving there, too.

We also saw why Bristol has been compared to Portland, Oregon. Green and hilly, the city is a center of art and alternative culture in England. In place of football fanaticism are hipsters and free-thinking rebels. It's where the bands Massive Attack and Portishead came out of, as well as one of my favorites, Idles. It's also where the street artist Banksy was born and got his start.

Sarah and I took a walk through his old neighborhood, along steep sidewalks bordered by rosebushes. We turned down a sleepy side street and found the stencil titled *Rose in a Mouse Trap* inconspicuously sketched on a long white wall. If the locals had not pitched in money to put a modest frame around it, I surely would have missed it.

A woman in her seventies parked her car adjacent to the artwork. No one was on the street except us. We made eye contact. "Good morning," Sarah said quietly, as the woman unloaded her groceries.

"Good morning, dear. Here to see the Banksy, are you?" She wore arty purple-framed glasses and a loose-fitting smock with lots of pockets, giving her the whimsical hippy vibe of Miss Frizzle from the *Magic School Bus* book series.

"It's that obvious?" I joked, evaluating my tourist uniform: Hoka shoes with sensible socks, sturdy pants, a rain jacket, and a backpack with snacks and water.

"Not a lot of people know, but that's where he lived," the woman told us, pointing out an innocuous house on the other side of the white wall. There was a small door at ground level that led into a courtyard. "There, in that garden apartment, with his girlfriend for a long time. Kept to himself, really. Just a nice young lad."

We thanked her for the insider information and kept walking up the hill. The high-perched row houses were each painted a different pastel color. We passed men and women who looked like they were part of a coven of wizards and witches. A man with muttonchops was smoking a pipe as he crossed the street in front of us, walking a great shaggy hound.

Coming down Spring Hill, the old-world charm slowly morphed into a vibrant, gritty part of Bristol. Almost every wall was covered in art. At a bustling intersection, we saw a mural covering the length and width of an entire building featuring a black woman with an Afro wearing a spacesuit. She raised her fist in protest. The caption "Bristol Rise Up" was sketched in the corner. During the Black Lives Matter movement that started after the murder of George Floyd, which happened close to my place of work in my hometown of Minneapolis, the protests that swept across America had eventually reached Bristol. In 2020, protesters in Bristol toppled the eighteen-foot statue of Edward Colston, a Bristol-based transatlantic slave trader, and threw it into the city harbor.

While crossing the street, we looked up at the right time and saw another Banksy. It was tucked behind a building and only visible from a certain angle. This one was titled *Mild Mild Mild West* and was of a teddy bear throwing a Molotov cocktail.

As we walked through this congested part of Bristol, I thought about another Banksy piece titled *There Is Always Hope*. A young child stretches her arm out as a heart-shaped balloon drifts away from her grasp. I could now easily see where Bansky got the sentiment from. This was a city where forces of good were trying to overcome a violent past and make a hopeful future. Though that feeling might not have been in the city's football stadiums, it was in its streets, and its people. It was on its walls. With Sarah by my side, hope, it seemed, was everywhere.

## CHAPTER SEVEN

# Brighton & Hove, East Sussex, January 22, 2024

The day after the Bristol City game, Sarah and I took the train to London and checked into an Airbnb near Hyde Park. Our slightly convoluted plan was as follows: after a morning with Sarah in London, I'd finally go see my favorite Premier League team, the Wolverhampton Wanderers, play an away game. I'd take a train an hour and a half from London to Brighton, see their 7:45 p.m. tilt against Brighton & Hove Albion FC, come back to London, and at 4 a.m. go with Sarah to Heathrow Airport to say goodbye.

So, the morning after we got to London, we went for a lovely walk through Hyde Park and had an early lunch at the chain restaurant Nando's, where even my meal was spiced up by English football: I dosed my PERi-PERi chicken with a sauce Nando's made in collaboration with Arsenal player Bukayo Saka. Then I was off to Brighton.

I found the seaside city to be snug and cozy, tucked into its winter offseason. The train station was quiet and orderly. A small number of passengers milled around and listened to a man noodle some chords on a rainbow-colored piano as they waited for their departures and arrivals. But this was only the quiet before the storm. I was early. An invasion of Midlanders, plus Todd from America, was steadily moving in like a low-pressure front. Out there, somewhere, a few thousand members of my tribe were coalescing.

Being an away supporter is one of the most intense parts of football fandom in England. In America, it's commonplace for fans of home and away teams to commingle. At Minnesota Timberwolves games, you'll often see Steph Curry jerseys in the lower bowl of the Target Center when the Warriors are in town. That would never happen in English football. Away supporters are physically separated from home club supporters not only by tradition but also by law.

Typically, the section away supporters are corralled into is known simply as the "away end." It is usually located behind a goal or wedged into a corner of a stadium's lower level, with walls or fencing or intentionally emptied stadium sections guarded by security personnel in high-visibility jackets. There are specific windows of time in which away supporters are allowed to enter the stadium. To access an away end, you use a dedicated entrance and exit that home supporters can't get to. Away supporters even have their own concession stands and bathrooms. Once you've entered the away end, there you will stay, confined to your area, prohibited from any other parts of the ground you may care to see. When the match ends, away supporters are often held in the stadium until all the home supporters have left.

I stayed put in the Brighton train station and watched it transform. Wolverhampton fans steadily piled in, while police put up metal barricades around us. At 5:45 p.m., two hours before kickoff, we were packed onto a local tram that took our roving horde to Brighton & Hove Albion's stadium. There, we were funneled toward our dedicated entrance through several barricades with tight switchbacks, manned by police with dogs. Drones hovered overhead. At the checkpoint, I presented my ticket—which I'd needed to prove official membership in the Wolverhampton supporters club to get. I spread out my arms and legs for a pat down.

I should have known how this search would go, but somehow, until I was asked to empty the contents of my Patagonia rain jacket's pockets, the ridiculousness of their contents hadn't struck me. I slowly removed each item, like my jacket was a clown car: cell phone, digital recorder, headphones, phone charger, notebooks, a stash of random pens, a small bottle of hand sanitizer, my passport, a grip of English pounds, and, embarrassingly, one of those large pill cases usually used by geriatrics for their daily medications, which elicited a few howls of *what the feck* from the Wolves supporters pouring in all around me. The security guard poked at each item with his inspection wand. The policeman and his dog perked up with curiosity at the sheer amount of shit spilling forth.

"I'm Todd from America," I explained. "I'm a writer."

"Okay?" the security guard said, shrugging. Then he poked his inspection wand at the pill case. He flipped it over. In addition to having Crohn's disease, I suffer from chronic migraines. Before leaving Minnesota, I'd self-administered injections of my meds for both conditions, one shot into each thigh. But I still needed the daily pills. The Monday-to-Sunday day slots rattled with my assorted gastrointestinal and migraine medications. It was all quite humiliating.

"Okay, you're good. Pick up your . . . items," the guard said. And off to the warm embrace of supporter jail I went, right where I belonged.

I entered the away end through a turnstile that was cut into the middle of a wall. I scanned my ticket, a green light lit up, and the bar clanged open.

"We . . . hate . . . Albion! We hate Albion!" my fellow away supporters chanted. I joined in. Our chanting leader was a chubby Kevin James type who stood in the middle of the away end concourse. Foot traffic swirled all around him, but he stood straight and strong, a beer-guzzling bulwark.

"We . . . hate . . . Albion! We hate Albion!"

An hour before game time, the Wolves supporters were already getting after it, drinking and chanting at full throttle. With the low concrete roof and hundreds of people singing in such a small space, the away end concourse was a cauldron of sound. My ears rang. My chest swelled. My brain tingled.

Many of the supporters had a real Dungeons & Dragons vibe. This tracked, because Wolverhampton is in the medieval stronghold of the Midlands region. During the Industrial Revolution it became coal mining country, the black lung of the United Kingdom. Wanderers supporters were not a cosmopolitan fan base like you'd find at Tottenham. These were proud people, but not pretty ones. There were a lot of balds. There was a lot of neck hair. There were a lot of men cupping meat pies and washing them down with great gulps of beer and roaring for more. I felt transported to the hovel pubs of yore.

These weren't the only type of Wolves fans, though. There were the John Oliver types, normal-looking blokes wearing glasses and old-school Adidas Gazelles. These harmless middle managers wore their allegiance to Wolves with vintage zip-ups and scarves, cool retro swag that told the world just how long they'd been supporting the club. After that, there were the more inimitable oddballs. I saw identical twins with bright ginger beards who were both wildly cross-eyed, which was somewhat alarming. There were two men in Wolves-themed turbans. There were lots of women in the mix, too, hardy and sensible, wearing practical jackets and chunky wool socks stuffed into Adidas Sambas.

At one point, English football legend Peter Crouch, a six-foot-seven stork of a forward who played for many different teams, none of which was Wolverhampton or Brighton & Hove, walked into the away end concourse. By all accounts he did so by accident, calling somewhat into question the tight security protocols I'd witnessed. He was as stunned as everyone else. Crouch is a great lad, famous for his abnormal physique and wit. When asked what he'd be if he wasn't a footballer, Crouch famously said, "A virgin." The Wolves fans started mocking him with a chant. He played along and waved and then got the fuck out of there.

The Kevin James guy soon started a new chant. This one was really naughty.

"One-two-three! Albian the bastards are shagging their sisters! Everywhere they go! Shagging their sisters! Everywhere they goooooooooo!!!!!!"

I'll admit, I thought it was funny. I was swept up in the communal Us versus Them feeling. Despite the fact that the Wolves were decidedly at the bottom of the table and on the cusp of relegation, and Brighton was a just a mid-table club, these supporters had traveled three hundred miles from home on a Monday for a night match and would get home barely before sunrise and be at work in the morning. They were here to give it hell.

In a brief pause in the chanting, an older man stepped forward right in front of me and began to sing a solo ballad. It was like a poignant scene in a movie, a calm point of tenderness for soldiers before the siege at dawn. His voice rose above the din, cutting through the chaos with the clarity of a trumpet in a royal announcement. The away end quickly quieted down in a sign of respect. As the man sang, unaccompanied, he kept his eyes closed.

> Fight, fight,
> Wherever you may be,
> We are the boys of the black country,
> And we'll beat you all wherever you may be,
> We are the boys of the black country

On that last line, the entire away end erupted in unison and joined in as a bombastic backing chorus.

My seat was directly on the barricade that separated the home and away supporters. The Wolves fans around me pressed in on my seat and gave an endless barrage of insults and wanker hand signs to the Brighton fans across the way. The Brighton supporters refused to partake, which only incensed the Wolves supporters more.

"Is this a library? Is this a library?" the away end chanted.

In fairness to the Brighton fans, it's hard to sing while holding your breath. From the start of the match, Brighton held possession for a huge majority of the time, forming buildups and attacks, but Wolves were well organized and weathered each one with a massive defensive posture, cheekily referred to as "parking the bus." Then, during the rare moments when Wolves had the ball, they hit Brighton on the break with sizzling tempo. The anxiety level among the Brighton fans looked high.

The level of skill and play from both squads was shocking to see up close. The speed with which the players in the English Premier League process the game both physically and mentally is what separates them from the other levels. The Bristol City versus Watford match I had just attended was technically only one level below the EPL, but now that I was here, I felt it might as well have been ten. It was like I'd gone from watching a black-and-white episode of *Leave It to Beaver* to the Technicolor of *Avatar*. The passes were delivered with an audible snap. The shots on goal were delivered with the tail spray of a rocket. The hard, crunching fouls were delivered with authority. Cross-field passes were pinged with the touch of a master archer. The Brighton midfielders were playing keep away with short, quick passes that were dizzying to watch. The Wolves attacker Pedro Nieto weaved and sprinted with the ball like an NFL punt returner.

Even Brighton midfielder James Milner, a thirty-eight-year-old warhorse making his 633rd professional appearance since he'd debuted for Leeds as a sixteen-year-old in 2002, looked downright agile and nimble. Brighton's academy and development of young talent, which has become world renowned in the last decade, was quite evident, too. Their young players ran tirelessly up and down the pitch, combining speed with precise passing.

The game was still knotted at 0–0 as the second half began. The Wolves were pressing. They desperately needed the points because they were circling the moon door to relegation, as Rog from *Men in Blazers* might say, in a reference to *Game of Thrones*. The anxiety was now high in both ends of the stadium. In place of heartfelt serenades and barbed comedy, the Wolves chants became distressed, delivered in guttural grunts. Speaking of *Game of Thrones*, a towering man with the grizzled look of Sandor "The Hound" Clegane punched the air with his chants, trying to push the Wolves players over the line. "COME ON WOLVES! STICK IN BOYS!" he goaded.

At the seventieth minute, with the action heating up and both teams going for the win, my phone buzzed with an alert.

**Your Return Train to London Tonight Has Been Canceled. Make Alternate Plans.**

Oh, that's not good, I thought. I'd promised Sarah I would be back in time to accompany her to Heathrow.

I pulled up the train app and saw that almost all the London-bound trains from Brighton after the game had been canceled, too, for reasons unknown. I would most likely have to take a train to some other place and then hope I could get from there to London. I decided to leave the game early. Though I might have been panicking beyond the point of necessity, I also felt I was seeing the basic idea clearly. Watching my Wolves finish out their game was important, but not as important as saying goodbye to Sarah.

There was just one problem, as the security guard by the exit soon reminded me. I was an away supporter in an away end. I wasn't allowed to leave.

After some pleading, the guard called over a police officer with a dog on a short leash. "What's this, then?" the policeman asked.

"My train was canceled, and I don't know how to get back to London," I said. "I'd like to leave and get to the train station as soon as possible."

He repeated the guard's explanation of why I couldn't. "Please," I begged weakly. "I'm Todd from America. Listen to my accent." I showed him my passport, and the alert about the train, and he relented.

"Okay," he said. "We will walk you to the tram station."

He and his dog escorted me as a drone followed above, making sure that I didn't stab anyone, incite a riot, or burn anything down. I got on the tram, arrived at the empty Brighton train station, and sprint-walked to the departure board. I didn't see a single train going back to London. But there was one called "the Gatwick Express" departing in a literal minute. I knew that Gatwick was an airport outside London, and figured it was close enough. I ran to the train and jumped on just as the doors were closing.

The ride was a fraught one for me. I kept waiting for a conductor to ask for my nonexistent ticket, shame me for being a stupid tourist, and kick me off. During the ride, I learned that the game had ended in a 0–0 draw. Not the ideal outcome, but at least Wolves had gotten a ranking point from it, and I hadn't missed much.

More luck came my way. After forty minutes the Gatwick Express stopped in London, at the Victoria Station, only a short Tube ride away from my Airbnb. And I had made it there without confrontation with a conductor. But the celebration was short-lived. Fate turned against me once more, putting me right back in another caged-in scenario. Police officers and station employees were huddled around the exit turnstiles, which I realized you needed to scan a ticket to get through. I was trapped.

Then I spotted a custodian on a floor sweeper moving toward an open gate connecting the platform I was on and the main part of the Tube station. Before I could chicken out, I sprinted through the open gate, boarded a train on the Tube line I needed, and was home free.

When I reached our Airbnb, I was sweating profusely. Sarah was joyfully watching *Gogglebox*, her favorite British reality show, and absentmindedly packing.

"How was the game?" she asked. "Anything fun happen?"

After an abbreviated night of sleep, Sarah and I got up and headed for Heathrow. It was a slobbering and tear-filled goodbye. Honestly, I wasn't quite sure I could pull this whole operation off without her. Even though we had mostly done our own things, we had traveled together for three weeks, and she was such a wonderful companion and grounding force to the chaos of my journey. At the end of every day, we'd come back together. She was my home base. Now I wondered if I'd be like an away supporter without a crew everywhere I went.

## CHAPTER EIGHT

# Westway Sports & Fitness Centre, North Kensington, West London, January 23, 2024

The day after Sarah left, I was feeling a little lonely and adrift. Thankfully, I had something to look forward to, which seemed like it might give me the sense of community and fellowship I was used to at home.

At the end of my disastrous attempt to use the Footy Addicts app a few weeks back and join a pickup soccer game in London, I'd noticed the neoprene-sleeve-and-braces-wrapped old men on another field. Among those wizened old men: that's where I belonged. So, I'd done some research and figured out that they were part of a group called the Freestylers. Their games were marked on the app as by invitation only, but I'd found the contact info for the host and written him a heartfelt email. He'd invited me to join.

So, I hoofed my way back to the Westway Sports & Fitness Centre in West London. I felt nervous standing outside the gate to the big field where I'd seen the Freestylers the last time. A man in his thirties with long hair and a blue Chelsea zip-up approached me and introduced himself, putting me at ease.

"My name is Alex," he said. "You must be the American playing with us tonight."

"Yes, I'm Todd from America. Great to meet you."

"Very nice to meet you, too," Alex said. We shook hands.

"A few weeks ago, I played over there," I told him, pointing toward the caged pitches under the motorway.

"Aha," Alex said with a knowing look. "We all started down there. Then we graduate to this game."

We walked out onto the pitch together. It was elevated, giving me a clear view of the A40 motorway. There were several digital billboards along it that were glowing in the murky night sky. Heavy mist gave the West London streets the look of a gritty neighborhood in a noir film.

Soon enough, all the Freestylers arrived. I met Tom, the host of the group who had received my message. "After I read your email, I knew you were one of us," he told me. The age range was thirties to sixties. Each man wore a kit from the club or country he supported. I wore a Hiawatha Supply work shirt because it was a gentle reminder to myself to put in a real shift.

"Here you go, Todd from America," a player named Jack said, as he kindly handed me a bib. "Great to have you, mate."

The men of this ragtag group were familiar to me. There was a guy in his thirties in a zipped-up jacket, sweatpants, and a stocking cap, who looked like he was trying to cut weight for a high school wrestling match. There was a towering center back with a GoPro camera on his chest. There was a stoic Croatian in an old-school national team kit who I instantly recognized as someone I didn't want to piss off. There was a miniature Michael Chiklis look-alike in Queens Park Rangers kit who had the body shape of a fire hydrant and a barbed Cockney accent that could strip paint. Before we even started playing, I could tell I'd found the Donkeys of West London.

I rooted into the left back position, the place on the field I've called home for decades. The ball was kicked into play, and I tried not to stick out. Every regularly scheduled pickup game of footy has its own idiosyncrasies that are particular to that location. Just like a coveted local surf break in Hawaii, each pickup game has quirks and codes of conduct. They're governed by the locals, and as a newcomer, it was in my best interest to not raise a fuss and just blend into the scenery and figure out the dynamics before I started trying to do or say anything notable. So I sat back and let the game play out for a bit.

These guys really knew how to play. Each man brought with him a bag of tricks and a deep knowledge of the game. The play moved at a steady but manageable clip. In the cages across the walkway, it had been all about raw strength and aggression. The Freestylers game was more cerebral. They relied on their brains and decades of experience. Whether their broken-down bodies could deliver the ball to the place they knew it should go or allow them to make the perfectly timed run they knew they should make . . . that was a whole different story. But the ideas were there!

Just as at home, these aging soccer players had tapped their collective histories with the game to grab something that most adults had lost along the way: a love for the golden art of pickup football. A player's individual work rate depended on his level of digestion and mood, his home life, his work life, his current injury status (note: we are all injured, all the time), and what he got into the night before. There was no more glory, only guts. These guys, like me, used foam rollers and straps and bands and little rubber balls with spiky nips and ointments and powders and witchcraft just to be able to get out on the field for one hour a week. At our age, attendance at the match was a victory in itself. Sure, a shot into the top bins or a perfectly weighted through-ball was great. But have you ever loafed around a skunked pitch on a Tuesday night at 9:00 p.m. and played through a balky hamstring and heartburn? That's legendary behavior.

Even though I didn't touch the ball for the first few minutes, I was having fun. I was serviceable and marked my man, tracked back, made countless runs, and supported the man with the ball. The pace slowed and holes began to open as the players got wheezy and a tad farty. The ball was on the far sideline with my teammate playing right back, and he moved it to the center back. Instinctively, I backpedaled to the far sideline near me to spread the field. I opened up for a pass.

This was my moment.

The center back played a hard pass to me. Water sprayed off the ball. As I opened up my body a little more to receive the ball on my trusty left foot, I chanted in my head, *Don't fuck it up, don't fuck it up.* I cradled the pass softly and quickly began to run forward. I was now in the game. I scanned my options and then zipped a pass between two opponents to a forward.

"Yes, Todd, yes," the man in the Croatia kit yelled encouragingly. A few minutes later, I pinged a ball to my teammate Jack, who was streaking down the far sideline toward the goal like a spooked deer tearing through an open field. "Yes, Todd, yes."

For the rest of the game, the Freestylers lit me up with positive encouragement: "Good ball there, Todd!" and "Keep going, son!" and "Good battle, Todd!" and "Great pressure, Todd from America!"

Toward the end of the game, I battled with an opponent on a 50/50 ball. I inadvertently knocked him down. I felt bad, but no foul was called and the game played on. As I moved up the field, my shame was palpable.

"Good stick, Todd," said Tom, the leader of the Freestylers. "No foul. Good battle."

I turned around and offered a hand to help my opponent up. He looked like Frank Zappa, with dark bushy eyebrows matched by a dark bushy mustache. He had a lot of rings on his fingers.

"Thanks, mate," the Frank Zappa look-alike said. "But I think I'll sit here for a bit."

After the game, I was invited to join the Freestylers at the Eagle, a local pub in North Kensington. The second I walked in it felt like I was in an episode of *Ted Lasso*. Every ounce of the heart and humor on that show was soaked into this special night. About a dozen Freestylers sat around a table in the back. We did not talk about the glory of the game, though. We did what all old athletes do when they get together. We talked about our injuries.

"My doctor told me last week that I should no longer play football," a Freestyler said, raising a pint glass. "Cheers to not taking that advice!"

Tom regaled us with a story of a recent bike accident. He had severe road rash all over his thigh and butt cheeks. The rash became infected, which resulted in a hospital stay.

"I was in St. Mary's Hospital in a wonderful part of London. A view of the Thames. It was all quite lovely. But the medical staff could not figure out how to fix my infected road rash. It was quite troublesome," Tom said. "Every hour for five days, a different staff member from a different medical department would come into my room to look at the rash. Every hour, I'd have to lift up my gown and show them my arse."

The lads began to hoot with laughter. Tom paused and took a pull from his pint. "There were so many different doctors looking at my arse that it got to the point where every time I heard the door open and the sound of the equipment trolley come in, I would just bend over and show them my arse," Tom said.

"Like Pavlov's dog," a Freestyler chirped from the end of the table to appreciative jeers.

"One night, I heard the door open and the sound of the trolley. I simply bent over and showed them my arse," Tom said. "But it was met with silence. I turned around with my arse still out and saw to my horror that it was the food man with my dinner!"

The table erupted. We ordered another round of pints.

It was one of the best nights of my trip, and it came at the perfect time. I had found a home here among my fellow Donkeys. If I ever lived in London, these were the guys I'd play footy with. The whole Freestylers scene was just a vibe, man. I liked it so much, in fact, that I rearranged some of my travel plans just so I could play with them a few more times.

The next day, I trained north to a town named Grimsby, and into the next part of my journey into the vast unknown of English football. On the way, I received two amazing texts. First, Sarah was back in America and thanked me for the gift of a month's worth of grilled chicken that I had cooked before we left and put in individually marked Tupperware and then frozen. Second, I received a message from Footy Addicts. The members of the Freestylers weekly pickup game had voted me Man of the Match.

## CHAPTER NINE

# Grimsby Town, Northeast Lincolnshire, January 24-27, 2024

I had heard all the warnings about Grimsby Town.

It was "real stabby," anecdotally, and the most violent city in Lancashire County, statistically. There was nothing there except drugs and a bad football team. It was literally voted the worst city in England.

I knew that expectations can shape reality. I didn't want to judge too quickly. But when the first thing I saw after dropping my bags at my Airbnb and going to the grocery store was a child on a leash eating popcorn off the floor while their parent looked at their phone, it was difficult to look past the cold hard truth.

I'd chosen to come to Grimsby because I wanted to see football played in a place that had lost the other thing that defined it. Grimsby was once home port to the world's largest fishing fleet. A 309-foot clock tower, a gift from Prince Albert, rose from the town docks as a beacon of strength and wealth. The Grimbarians, as they're called, took immense pride in their successive generations of native sons who risked their lives in the dangerous North

Sea to feed their nation. The threat of dying or being injured in their work was so real that when the sailors reached shore and got paid, they were known as "Three-Day Millionaires" because they blew all of their fortunes in epic runs of debauched gratitude. Once it became possible to preserve fresh fish in ice and transport it by rail, fish caught by Grimbarians in the morning would show up in London restaurants that night. It was the haul brought in by these men that helped usher in the craze for the country's iconic dish, fish and chips.

Due to a myriad of factors—international fishing disputes, overfishing, labor shortages, bad government policies—the fishing industry and its jobs were eventually pulled clean out of Grimsby like the swift deboning of a northern Atlantic cod. By the 1980s, Grimsby suffered mass unemployment. The jobs never returned.

I was curious if that history would make the town's football club a more important focus of its residents—a shared thing to rally around—or a secondary concern when there was so much else to worry about. Grimsby Town FC, est. 1878, were competitive through their first few decades, often beating teams fielded by much larger cities. From the start, they featured a trawler boat and fish on their team crest. Their peak moments came between 1929 and 1939, when they played the vast majority of their games in the top division of English football and made it to the semifinals of the FA Cup twice. After that, their performance was spotty. They became what's known as a "yo-yo club," swinging up and down through the different levels, in all switching divisions thirty-two times, with fifteen promotions and seventeen relegations. At the moment, they were in the fourth-tier League Two, with a real possibility of getting relegated again at the end of the season.

The day I arrived, Grimsby Town FC's Under-18 team had an evening match. Youth clubs of this nature are known as academies—in American terms, it would be like a cross between an elite high school team and a farm team for a professional baseball club. I regrouped at my Airbnb after the grocery store and got ready for the game. First, I needed to pause in the vestibule of my flat while a man out on the street was having a psychotic event. I waited until there was a break in the yelling. Then I made it onto a bus, on which I rode with two women in tattered down coats who carried mop buckets with loaves of bread sticking out of them.

The bus dropped me off a few blocks away from Blundell Park, the stadium where the youth and senior teams both play. The legendary ground has been Grimsby Town FC's home since 1898. As I walked, I could smell the sea. The stadium's front gate rose out of the darkness like the Black Gate of Mordor from *The Lord of the Rings*. The walls were thick and metal and painted black and had spikes and barbed wire strung across the top in a lattice pattern.

Inside, things were far less intimidating. It was a proper old English ground, a relic to a humble and simpler time of football, and I absolutely loved it. There were no frills here, no modern amenities. Metal roofs hung low over three of the four sections. Wood beams and cheap plastic seats spoke to a bygone architecture and aesthetic. The bathrooms were fortresses seemingly built to survive the blitzkrieg. There was a pub underneath one of the stands. The walls were adorned with framed pictures of long-ago teams: the players in short shorts, long socks, and billowy black-and-white striped kits.

The U18 game I was there to see was meaningful to the town on two major counts. It was an FA Youth Cup match, and one against a higher-level opponent. Millwall FC played in the second-tier Championship division. The Grimsby boys had beaten the youth team of Premier League side Nottingham Forest to get here, and if they could pull off a second straight upset, it would be a big deal. However, the mood before the match was not at all celebratory, and for good reason. Grimsby Town U18 were playing their first game since the tragic deaths of their popular defender Cameron Walsh and his father, Dave, in a car accident.

The team warmed up in white T-shirts adorned with Cameron's face. The crowd of supporters around me watched while talking low and taking long, contemplative pulls from their tea and coffee and pints. The stands were nearly full—impressive, I thought, for a Wednesday night in horrid weather. Sheets of mist blew in off the Humber Estuary a quarter of a mile away. Perhaps football was helping to bring a struggling fan base in mourning together. I stood along the field and watched warm-ups from a sideline railing.

An older man with a round face, chappy hat, and bulbous nose was next to me. He looked something like the cartoon mascot from the Andy Capp's Hot Fries packaging. We nodded hello to each other.

"Terrible thing that happened to that young lad. 'Tis just terrible," he said.

"Yes, tragic," I agreed.

"Say, where you from, then?"

"I'm Todd from America."

"Bob," he said, shaking my hand. "What state are you from, then?"

"Minnesota."

"Is that a Trump state, then?"

This question came up all the time. After learning that I was American, almost everyone I met wanted to know if I was from a Trump-supporting state or not. I would find myself wondering which answer they were hoping for, and tried to avoid politics as best as I could. The people of Grimsby had decidedly voted for Brexit and supported Boris Johnson—the conservative politician often compared to Trump—for prime minister. Johnson had even been photographed multiple times in a Grimsby Town FC hat. I told Bob that Minnesota was a purple state, explaining what that meant and flailing for an off-ramp joke about Prince. It was good enough to get us to move on.

After some small talk about American television shows and the Grimsby Town FC senior team and the purpose of my trip, I asked Bob the question most on my mind. "Did you know the young player who died? Or know his dad?"

"I didn't know them. But I'm a Grimer," Bob said. He paused for a long while, and I tried to give him space. It seemed like he was searching for the right thing to say. "I *used* to come here," he continued. His words were uneasy and tottering, like the steps of a baby deer learning how to walk. He took a breath. Then he said, "I used to come here. I used to come to every Town game, home and away. I did that for a long time. I did that for far too long."

I looked over at Bob. He stared straight ahead at the field, but I could see tears welling up that were too stubborn to fall. I didn't quite know what to do. The heaviness of the night was so palpable there between us. The crowd behind us swayed and swelled as kickoff approached. I stayed still.

"I used to come here," he repeated. "I used to go to every Town home and away match. I was going to all the matches and carrying on in the pubs. Things, you know, mate, went that way for too long. I tried to get better. But I couldn't stop. I tried to get on with it. It was so hard to quit. I had to stop coming here. To get better."

Because of my Crohn's disease and migraines, I stopped drinking more than twenty years ago. Before that, I was a social drinker, not a very heavy one. In the time since, I've only had about four drinks, and all of them had been in the last four weeks. But I've known many alcoholics and addicts in my life. I've worked with them on blue collar jobs and counted them among my friends and family. I've been there in moments when life triggers something deep inside them and it unexpectedly rises to the surface. I told Bob: "Well, I'm glad you came tonight."

He nodded, keeping his eyes straight ahead. "Thanks, mate. It just felt right to come back. With what happened with this young man, I felt the need to come back. I wanted to show my support. I wanted to show support for Town. I wanted to show support for my old club."

Our conversation continued on in fits and starts until an announcement was made about Cameron Walsh and his father, Dave. Bob and I joined the entire stadium in a full minute of applause to honor their lives. When it ended, Bob turned toward me, his eyes still wet. He shook my hand and said, "Safe travels on your journey, mate." He blended into the crowd and was gone.

Grimsby Town U18 held Millwall off until late in the game, when, seemingly emotionally spent, they conceded a goal.

The game ended at 9:30 p.m. I trudged to a bus stop. I stood there alone, wet and shivering, feeling a little down. I had three more full days in Grimsby, with another football game only falling on the last one. I wondered what else this town would show me. I wondered if I could handle it.

The next day, I put on a brave face and walked the city. The decaying urban architecture reminded me of Rust Belt towns like Gary, Indiana; Akron, Ohio; and Flint, Michigan. A lot of the shops that were shuttered looked like they weren't coming back. Near my Airbnb was a pedestrian mall where a pack of small children on large mountain bikes did wheelies, sending me and everyone else in sight scattering and hugging the walls of the storefronts. I saw scrawny and itchy men with cold eyes and neck tats, slugging cans of energy drinks or beer and blowing great clouds of vape smoke. I crossed paths with a man outside a pawnshop who had a face tattoo and a pit bull on an extremely short leash.

I walked to a museum dedicated to the history of the town and the lives of trawlermen called the Fishing Heritage Center. There, I learned that in better times, many of the boats in Grimsby's massive fleet were named after English football clubs. I thought that was fun, until I got to the display dedicated to the sinking of the *Leicester City*. In 1953, it ran aground and capsized. Seven men died, eleven survived, all of them Grimbarians. A round life preserver from the vessel with the words "Leicester City" stamped on it was the last thing I saw as I exited the museum.

Through a contact at *The Cod Almighty*—a Grimsby Town FC fanzine whose staffers I'd gotten in touch with while planning my trip—I had signed up for shifts at the Rock Food Bank in the blighted East Marsh neighborhood. I was assured that if I wanted to meet the real people of Grimsby, this would be the place to do it.

So, the next morning, at 6:15 a.m., I walked to the food bank under a bright moon. I wore my steel-toed boots, double-knee work pants, a black work hoodie, and my Clapton CFC stocking cap. Next door to the food bank, I noticed a huge Grimsby Town FC flag on the wall behind the main counter of the A. R. Needham Butcher Shop.

I was assigned to ride in a cargo van and help gather food from various donors around town. My colleague and driver for the day, John, was a retired firefighter and an old bull of a worker of blunt disposition. Soon, we were off to the loading docks and back rooms and coolers of a series of grocery stores. John directed me as I pushed carts and hauled boxes. He was known in every store we went to as a man who got shit done in a timely manner. I followed suit.

Next, we drove out to the famous Grimsby docks. We were buzzed into a huge industrial warehouse full of frozen food and asked to wait for the boss. There was a command room up front with a dozen rubber boots stuck upside down on pegs to dry. There was a long coat rack that stretched the entire length of the wall and had nothing but rain slickers and hard hats and high-visibility gear on it. There were signs everywhere with rules and regulations and warnings about the various dangers of dock work. I liked this kind of place. I was familiar with it. It wasn't so different from my Hiawatha Supply yard back home.

"You here to pick up the bacon?" a man said, approaching us. I was shocked: he was my doppelganger. Same age, same height, same build, a black hoodie, double knee work pants, steel-toed boots, and a black stocking cap with Liverpool FC's logo on it. He also wore the same goofy look on his face that I wear at Hiawatha Supply, the one that tells the world, "I'm in charge here, even though I don't really know what's going on, but I'll give it a go."

"Yeah," John said, introducing himself and then me as his apprentice from America.

"I'm Jimmy," said the boss. "America, mate? What are you doing here?"

"I'm writing a book about football. I'm here to see Town play on Saturday. I thought I'd put in a shift of work while I'm here. Help out where I could," I said. I looked at his hat and added, "I'm focusing on relegation."

"Well, you've come to the right place for that," Jimmy said. I wasn't sure if he was talking about the team or the town.

Jimmy led us into a cooler with white metal walls. He pointed to a pallet with shrink-wrapped boxes stacked six feet high. "This one here is yours."

"That's a lot of bacon," John said.

There was a pallet jack in the corner. I've been working pallet jacks since I was sixteen so was going to offer to man it. But this was Jimmy's dojo. He stepped up, and in one fluid motion he moved the jack and had the pallet levitating across the room. He was a true magician.

John, the old bull, sat back and let us two donkeys load the bacon into the van. Jimmy and I got along famously. I told him all about my travels so far, including my time at Goodison Park. His face twisted into a playful grimace.

"Everton is building the nicest Championship Division stadium in the league," he said, smirking.

I wasn't certain it was smart to talk shit on the Grimsby docks, but I felt like we had a vibe, so I let it fly. "Your Liverpool striker Darwin Nunez couldn't hit the ocean from the beach," I said.

"There you go." Jimmy laughed. "Now you got the hang of it."

Back at the food bank, I popped into the butcher shop during my lunch break to ask about the flag they had so prominently mounted on the wall. An older woman in a white butcher's coat was restocking some steaks in a glass case. "Excuse me," I said quietly. "I don't mean to interrupt. But can I ask you a question when you have a moment?"

"Go on, love," she said.

"I was just wondering why you have a Grimsby Town Football Club flag on your wall," I asked.

"Hold on, love," she said. She turned toward a door at the back of the shop and shouted, "HEY, DAVE!"

An older man in a white butcher's coat of his own shot out seconds later. He had thin hair, bushy eyebrows, and jigsaw teeth.

"Dave Needham," the butcher said, shaking with a hand that felt as solid and uncompromising as a shovel head.

"Todd from America," I replied. "Is this your shop?"

"Yes, I started working here for my dad when I was eight years old." He proudly walked me over to a framed picture on the wall. "Here we are." Dave and his dad, Archie, rosy-faced with a great cloud of white hair, posed together in front of an object I couldn't quite make out.

"I assume you're a big supporter of Town?"

"HAAAHAHAHA," cackled the woman behind the counter, witchlike. "This man knows everything about Grimsby Town Football."

Dave undid the top two buttons of his white coat and pulled out his tie. It had the team logo all over it. "We've supported Town my whole life. It was my dad's team and it is mine now. He started this business and then I took over. We've been Town our whole lives."

"Dave, just take Todd from America upstairs and show 'im your office," the woman said.

"Would you like to see my office?" Dave asked me.

I looked at the woman. "Would I?"

"You would, love," she said, winking.

I followed Dave up a staircase to the second floor. We passed a room with cold metal tables and bone saws and assorted other meat-cutting equipment. For a moment, I wondered if I'd just entered a horror movie. Was this the day I was either going to die or kill a man? But the fear passed as soon as Dave led me into his office.

In front of me was a privately held, postage stamp–sized Grimsby Town FC museum. Every available inch of the office was covered in memorabilia. There were framed newspapers from famous games and framed kits and stacks of programs and team photos and player photos and posters and other artifacts.

"This article is from 1930 when Town played the mighty Everton and their star striker Dixie Dean, one of the greatest strikers in English football history," Dave said, pointing to a framed newspaper. "We won four-nil. Dixie didn't get on the score sheet that match, but our local lad Robson scored a hat trick."

He moved a few feet over and pointed to another framed newspaper.

"This is from 1939 when we played Wolves in the FA Cup at Old Trafford," Dave said. "We set the attendance record with seventy-six thousand fans. The entire town emptied to go to the match."

I leaned in for a closer look. The opening graph of the newspaper article read, "As war clouds gather over Europe, Grimsby Town stood on the verge of Wembley glory."

A few feet over, Dave pointed to a framed article from January 4, 1986, about a home match between Grimsby and Arsenal. "Look closely at the background of the picture," he said. There were advertisements with a hand-painted look on the roof of the stadium. In the middle was a large sign for Needham Butchers. "Dad advertised at Blundell Park for a long time. He was so loved at the club and in the community that they named a meat pie after him."

"A meat pie? Now, that's an honor, especially for a butcher," I said.

"I'd say," Dave said, raising his eyebrows.

Above two small windows, there were two framed pictures of trawler boats. Dave walked over and pointed to one that was listed to its side. "That's the trawler named *Leicester City*," he said.

I knew it from the museum. "It shipwrecked, right?" I said.

Dave looked surprised. "Yes. My dad was on it," he told me.

"What?" I asked, flabbergasted.

"My dad, Archie, survived the wreck of the *Leicester City*," Dave said. "He was sixteen years old in 1953 and working as a galley boy. My grandmum had to pick one of her sons to go on the trawler. That's the way it was back then. Every man and young boy had to take a turn at sea. She picked my dad because he was a better swimmer than his brother. My dad learned how to swim from Brenda Fisher. She used to swim the English Channel."

"This is unbelievable," I said.

"The *Leicester City* was returning home to Grimsby after a long trip out at sea. It was near the tip of Scotland, close to the Orkney Islands, when they ran aground. The seven men that died either drowned or died of exposure to the cold water. My dad swam for days on end. Around and around. The fog was so thick he couldn't see land. Then a woman stood on the shoreline with a lantern. My dad swam to the light. A lot of good men died that day. Men from here. From Grimsby. My dad swam to the light and lived."

On my way out of the shop, I took another look at the picture of Dave and his dad. The objects they were posing in front of, the ones I hadn't been able to make out, were suddenly clear to me. Between them was a round life preserver with "Leicester City" stamped on it.

Something clicked for me. This was a place that had known so much loss and hardship, and isolation and relegation. It's also a place of survival, of getting on with it, head down, face to the wind and waves. In Grimsby, you keep swimming or you die.

The following day, I returned to Blundell Park to see Grimsby Town FC play a match against the Tranmore Rovers. Both teams were fighting to stave off relegation. The day and time was Saturday at 3:00 p.m., naturally.

I stood outside the Black Gates of Mordor waiting for two lifelong supporters who were also contributors to *The Cod Almighty*. They had generously gotten me a ticket to the match and agreed to host me. But I had no idea what they looked like.

"Are you Mark? Are you Jase? You're not perhaps waiting for Todd from America, are you?" I nervously asked several groups of strangers. None of them were. Finally, I approached a pair of men. One was hardy and stout, with a salt-and-pepper beard. The other was clean-cut and smiley.

"Todd from America?" they asked.

"YES!" I said.

"Welcome to Town!" the bearded one said. "I'm Mark!"

"I'm Jase!" said the other. We all shook hands and both men warmly clapped me on the back. Already, I was feeling comfortable again. Even in Grimsby, where my trip hadn't always been smooth, I was being welcomed into a new tribe.

"Ready for some pints?" Jase asked.

"Sure, sounds great," I said. Perhaps I wasn't so comfortable after all. I felt Grimsby wasn't a place for some soft-ass teetotaler.

The lads took me over to the fan zone, which at Blundell Park consisted of a few picnic tables next to the base of one of the floodlight towers and a single truck selling local beer and ciders. People seemed to be enjoying it, though. There was a family-reunion, everyone-knows-everyone kind of feel.

"My story, my life, has all happened here at Blundell Park," Mark told me as he handed me a pint of cider. "Growing up near here, I started riding my bike to my grandparents' house close by. Then I'd walk here and meet friends. And in adulthood that continues." We clinked our plastic cups together.

"Cheers," I said, sipping the cider. It was cold and crisp and delicious.

"It's more than just a team. This is our community hub," Jase said. I looked around again and could see and hear people welcoming each other. "We see people here every week and weekend. We have built these relationships for years. For seasons. Every Saturday at 3:00 p.m., we have a place to be and see each other and watch some football."

"That's a lovely thing, man," I said.

"When Town does well, the community does well. When Town struggles, the community struggles," Jase added.

After a few minutes of slagging off on the English Premier League and how its money-grubbing tentacles have destroyed so much of English football, Mark left to get another round of drinks. At one point, I had a pint in each hand. I'd gotten comfortable again. Mark and Jase were such great hosts and didn't pressure me to drink at all. I was just having a "When in Rome" moment, and it felt awesome.

We went into the stadium and took our seats high up in a section among a small group of supporters who worked on *The Cod Almighty*. The afternoon light was perfect. The game began, and each member of the *Cod Almighty* family fell into their designated role. A woman named Sue was the matriarch, wise and steady, and her comments were precise as drone strikes. Tony was a human computer of Grimsby Town FC history and spit out facts and records and provided statistical analysis. Jase sat with his arms crossed and was funny and smiling, taking in all the suckage and glory in equal measure, genuinely just happy to be there. Mark was the fun uncle, offering comedic relief. It was direly needed because the game was complete dog shit.

Both Grimsby and Tranmere were at the bottom of the League Two table and played like it. The match was incredibly boring and painful to watch because the players were scared of making a mistake that could result in relegation.

"It'd be a lot better if we had a midfield on the pitch. But apparently, we decided to not start one today," Mark joked. "Can we vote for an un-man of the match? . . . In the last three games, we've given up fourteen goals and scored six goals. We sacked a manager for it. A manager who is now doing quite well at something called Shrewsbury or whatever the feck."

After Grimsby conceded the match to Tranmere on a game-winning own goal, Jase sighed. "I'm afraid that Todd from America is getting the true Grimsby Town experience," he said.

If only that had been the end of it. After the match, we went out for fish and chips. The craic was excellent. But unfortunately, the mix of the cider and the excessively large platter of fried food worked like a bunker-busting bomb in my body. As soon as I got to my Airbnb I rushed to the bathroom and was sick from both ends for hours. Eventually I wanted to lie down in bed, but I was terrified of *literally* shitting it. I envisioned the Airbnb host's review of what I'd done to her "Live, Laugh, Love"–type flat, and the merciless British tabloids picking up the incident and it going viral and me becoming known worldwide as the infamous "Grimsby Town Shitter." So, I did what any reasonable man would do: I put on a swimsuit over my boxer briefs, like a homemade diaper.

At dawn, I dragged myself to the Grimsby train station. A shredded and soiled Union Jack flag flapped lazily in the wind, a stark reminder of how far this town has fallen from its heyday as a bustling port of a proud island nation. The train station doors were unexpectedly locked. A cluster of passengers loitered outside and quickly became indignant. A police officer arrived and milled through the crowd and took in every passenger's face. He clutched a printout with a mugshot on it. Jase was right after all. This was the authentic Grimsby experience.

I couldn't wait to leave.

CHAPTER TEN

# Liverpool to Craven Cottage, Fulham, West London, January 28-31, 2024

I had always planned for a couple of days of rest and relaxation after Grimsby. I would go to York, one of England's most tranquil cities. I would take long, peaceful walks amid the thirteenth-century Gothic cathedrals and the high street reminiscent of Diagon Alley from *Harry Potter.* My only work assignment would be a gentle one: covering a York City Football Club academy game at their quaint stadium. After the local ciders and fish and chips of Grimsby had turned my insides out, I was looking forward to this more than ever.

That's not what happened. Instead, I went back to Liverpool. Then I took a four-and-a-half-hour bus ride to West London with the most die-hard Everton supporters, watched a night game, and took an only slightly quicker middle-of-the-night bus back with them. Was it a good choice for my depleted system? It was not. Did I regret it? Not in the least.

The offer to join the Toffee away supporters came from Graeme Davies, the young man I'd spent the day with at Goodison Park, and it was too awesome to resist. I plugged myself with Imodium, drank loads of electrolytes, took my migraine meds, and got on the damn bus.

Actually, there were *nine* buses of Scousers, driving in a caravan. On mine were not only Graeme but his father, Thomas—the man with the foghorn voice who sold game-day programs at Goodison Park. We were making good time, which would be a positive on most road trips, but not for us. We were ordered to pull over and kill time at the truck stop because we were on pace to arrive too early for our away supporter–designated entrance window at Craven Cottage, home of Fulham FC.

It was at the truck stop that I learned what it truly means for an apple not to fall far from a tree. The lot was packed with motorists stretching their legs, and freezing cold. Thomas, an old ironside, gave zero fucks. He wanted to show me the twenty-three tattoos covering his entire back and stripped off his clothes to do so. Each was of the face of a different Everton football player. They were aligned in symmetrical rows like school portraits in a yearbook.

After a few obligatory words of admiration, I asked what I really wanted to know. "Do you regret getting any of them?"

"Only one," Thomas gamely answered. "Duncan Ferguson."

Ferguson was an Everton legend. His bleeding face was on a mural adjacent to Goodison Park. "How come?" I asked.

"I met him once and told him that I had his face tattooed on my back. He said I was mental!" I wasn't about to tell Thomas this, but I'd have to side with Ferguson.

It wasn't just the tattoos, though. This whole away trip was mental.

The ten-point deduction Everton had received in punishment for claims of financial misconduct, paired with its highly mediocre on-field play, was keeping the team right on the edge of the relegation zone. They were in seventeenth place out of twenty. If they dropped to eighteenth or lower and stayed there, out of the Premier League they would go. Everton gaffer Sean Dyche said managing the club was like "juggling sand."

Trying to stave off a relegation threat gives fans something to cheer for, but despite Graeme's love for the Toffees, this was not a fun team to watch. Everton's lead striker, Dominic Calvert-Lewin, hadn't scored in fifteen games. The Fulham team they were playing wasn't a whole lot more interesting. Their records were almost identical, though they were in a more secure position at the moment without the ten-point penalty.

But hey, I thought, this is what I was here to do: get a little mental. It's the name of the game for the most passionate English football supporters. They wouldn't have it any other way. They want a good fight. They stick in and see what's what.

Back on the bus, I was sitting next to Graeme when news broke that Everton's appeal to the point reduction would be heard in the next few days with the results coming a few weeks later. So, there was a small amount of hope on the horizon that the club could at least get a few points back, which might help them get to safety.

Graeme reacted with a mix of positivity and grousing about the Premier League's corruption. It reminded me of the protest flag I'd held the corner of in Goodison Park. I'd been certain, since then, that Graeme was a member of the secretive 1878s—the underground organizing body of anti-EPL Everton supporters—but I hadn't confirmed it with him directly. This seemed an opportune moment.

A huge smile opened up across Graeme's face when I posed the question. "Yes, mate. I'm part of the group."

"I feel like I just unmasked Batman," I said.

"Well, the Batman with Robert Pattinson was filmed in Liverpool."

"You know, in six months of trying, I never received a single reply from the 1878s," I told him. "Now here I am, sitting next to *the guy* on a bus going to an away match. Fucking hell, dude. Unreal."

"So, now you have me," Graeme said. "What do you want to know?"

I peppered Graeme with questions about the activities of the guerilla resistance group. He told me about the protest marches he'd helped organize and the placards and banners and flags that I saw in the stands. It seemed like Graeme really *was* Batman. But he was a part of a Justice League of fighters.

"There was one banner that said, 'You Messed with the Wrong Club and the Wrong Fans.' That was you?" I asked.

"Not just me. It was the 1878s. But yes. That was us. They tried to get rid of us. But we shall not be moved," Graeme said, referencing another banner that the 1878s prominently fly in Goodison Park on match days.

The final stretch of the drive through West London to Craven Cottage was quite lovely. The money was on clear display. There were long blocks of well-maintained houses with arched doorways over heavy front doors ornately decorated with stained glass. Small wreaths and garlands adorned the fronts of the houses. Luxury vehicles lined the streets. Pedestrians were well groomed and cheery and had full sets of teeth, a stark departure from Liverpool and Grimsby.

Craven Cottage rose right out of the neighborhood. Opened in 1896, it's the oldest football stadium in London. The historic Johnny Haynes Stand was designed by the noted Scottish engineer and architect Archibald Leitch and is a Grade II listed building protected by English Heritage.

Everything about the building spoke to a different era. It resembled a giant field house with its brick and stone facade and ornate windows and spires, a building that could easily house the Triwizard Tournament at Hogwarts. Every touch of brick, every panel of wood, and every pane of leaded glass was pure class. The turnstiles for the home supporters were thin and ancient. Stanchions of floodlights illuminated the area. As we disembarked from the bus, the air was warmer than I'd expected.

The away end entrance was in the corner of the stadium immediately adjacent to the actual cottage at Craven Cottage. The security and police presence was shockingly light, not at all like my experience with the Wolves fans in Brighton. I was wearing a blue Everton hat Graeme had bought me.

"Tennis fans and Tories around here," Graeme said, eyeing the Fulham crowd on our way in. He had a point: they looked WASPy, like bros from Connecticut, lots of finance guys and well-heeled adults in scarves and vests and tailored jackets. "They're not going to do fuck-all with us. They know they don't want any part of this Everton lot."

I moved freely into the away end. To my pleasant surprise, there was no cage, no barbed wire, and nothing restricting our movements here. It was almost like a night off for the traveling Everton supporters. They weren't digging in and preparing for battle. There was no decades-old animosity between Everton and Fulham. The air felt clear.

As Graeme and I worked our way through the crowd, I heard the telltale sign of the Americanization of an EPL club: the ubiquitous jock rock song "Seven Nation Army" by the White Stripes. This tracked because Fulham is owned by Shahid Khan, the billionaire owner of the Jacksonville Jaguars of the NFL and All Elite Wrestling. He was a man who knew how to cater to American interests. He's not alone: Americans now own approximately half of all Premier League teams. Khan had recently released plans to make Craven Cottage more like EverBank Stadium in Jacksonville. He wanted to build a rooftop pool, party deck, and nightclub on the historic ground.

My seat was halfway up behind the goal, right in the heart of the away end. Graeme was to my right and Thomas, thankfully now clothed, was to my left. The opening whistle sounded, and in seconds the white haired, gentle-seeming grandpa type next to Thomas turned into a raving Scouser. A lineman's arm went up signaling an Everton player was offside and he yelled, "Feck off, you twat!" Everton had a shot on Fulham's goal that was cleared off the line, missing a much-needed goal by literal centimeters, and Grandpa yelled, "Get in, you fecking bastard!"

The Fulham support was milquetoast at best. There was hardly any chanting or singing coming from the home crowd. Loads of the fans were using hand clappers, which was weird. When a group of Fulham fans a section over decided it would be fun to chirp the Everton supporters, they were met with expletives so hot and explosive it reminded me of the scene in *Apocalypse Now* where the tree line explodes in a ball of fire. The Fulham supporters had brought a baguette to a knife fight. The grandpa led the counter-attack by flipping the reverse peace sign that meant "stick it up your arse" while yelling, "You Tory cunts!"

During this hot pot of Scouse stew, a massive individual with a ginormous bald head and the domineering gangster presence of the Spiderman villain Kingpin was in front of me. The back of his skull was tattooed with the Everton logo. He didn't speak a word, he just menacingly eyed the Fulham crowd.

We stood the whole time the ball was in play, of course. Then at halftime, we simply sat down. This is the tradition of most Everton supporters. They are so locked into the game that they don't waste time on refreshments or concessions or even going to the bathroom. They rest their legs but keep their head and voice in the game, warm and ready, like an idling engine. I turned to Thomas and took the opportunity to keep my voice in tune by asking him about his illustrious past as an Everton away supporter.

"I've been attending matches at Goodison Park for fifty-six years," he told me. "I was taken by my father, and to be honest, it was love at first sight. The rest, as they say, is history."

"When was your first away match?"

"Eighth of November 1975," he said, as easy as reciting his birth date. "I was still at school and attended the game with a school friend who was also an Evertonian. It was a time when football hooliganism was rife, so for a youngster of fifteen years of age, it was quite a frightening experience. Everton lost the game three to two. By this time, I was well and truly hooked. Unbelievable as it may sound, I traveled to and from the game, gained admission, and bought a match magazine all-inclusive for under one pound.

"Back in the mid-seventies, away fans were treated like cattle," he continued. "The police and the football fan were far from friendly with each other. Hostile, you could say. The police could also be very brutal if trouble on the terraces broke out. Hooliganism and violence were a regular feature on a Saturday afternoon. You took your life in your own hands when you went to away matches."

"The word on the street is that you were a part of Everton's legendary Road to Rotterdam when they won the 1985 European Cup," I said.

"Yes, I was there," Thomas said. "I went to a game in Bratislava in October 1984 when it was still Czechoslovakia. It was what they called 'going behind the Iron Curtain.' When we arrived, all the hotels were fully booked. We had to be off the streets by 22:30 due to the curfew. The police and army were out on patrols looking to beat supporters. We played cat and mouse for hours. Trying to catch some sleep in the bathrooms and train stations before the police showed up. We ended up resting overnight in a field."

"What makes you want to travel the world supporting Everton?"

"You always hear supporting a football club described as an addiction or obsession," Thomas said. "I think there's some truth to that. For me, this was my club. It has been since I was a boy. That addiction or obsession feeling comes from me not wanting to miss a moment. There's always a chance for a great win by the club or a great play or a great goal by a player. I wanted to be there to see it. I didn't want to miss anything."

I heard this a lot. The chance to bear witness to a great football moment from your club is a large part of what fuels the drive to attend the away match. That craving can be stronger than the need for sleep or work or relationships. Away supporters can't stomach the thought of missing a moment so great it becomes immortalized in a song or chant that will be sung for generations.

In the second half, Fulham put the Everton defense under constant pressure. The most important players in back were Everton's James Tarkowski, a veteran with a workman's fortitude that made him like a human forklift, and Jarrad Branthwaite, a promising young defender with a tall, sleek physique whose stellar play recently had resulted in a call-up to England's national team. As Fulham's attack darted all around them, they orchestrated the defense with a combination of grace and fluidity. Fulham hit the woodwork several times, and the pressure was dialed up even further with every passing minute.

The English Premier League was, once again, a marvel to see up close. The rampaging speed of Fulham's American defender Antonee Robinson as he ran the sideline was insane to witness up close; João Palhinha, Fulham's midfield battle tank who was also Spain's national team starting midfield, never missed a single tackle, never made a bad pass, never made the wrong decision; and Calvert-Lewin, eager and hungry to break his drought, cracked a header off the Fulham bar. The 0–0 dogfight was a cagey, entertaining tilt that saw the teams combine for a whopping forty-six shot attempts.

To compound the nerves in the Everton away end, another team near the bottom of the table, Luton Town, had just shockingly beaten Brighton 4–0. This pushed Everton squarely into eighteenth place and the relegation zone. Especially if the appeal against the points deduction didn't go their way, conceding a late goal here at Craven Cottage could be the thing looked back on as what set the dominoes in motion to kill their entire season. All of Everton's bad luck and bad form over the last three years was palpable in the away end.

Then Everton's greatest fear arrived at the feet of Fulham's Willian, a Brazilian midfielder with balletic ball skills. He attacked from the wing and got inside Everton's goal box. Dwight McNeil, Everton's left-footed midfielder nicknamed McMessi for his late-game heroics, stepped in to defend Willian. McNeil was a solid player, but this matchup was grossly suboptimal. Willian deked out McNeil so badly he made him slide completely out of position, as if McNeil were wearing roller skates. Willian was now free to cross the ball into the six-yard box. In that second that Willian stood with the ball and McNeil slid toward the end line, every Everton away supporter simultaneously screamed in agony.

Willian's cross curled into the box so perfectly and with so much purpose it was as if its destiny was predetermined. The ball moved in slow motion, unimpeded, toward its inevitable conclusion, which was the yawning forehead of Fulham's six-foot-five center back Tosin Adarabioyo. The ball arrived, and Adarabioyo jumped and thumped it toward the far upper right corner.

Then came the kind of moment that we had all hoped we would witness. The kind of thing that could turn around a game, turn around a season, be talked about for years.

Everton goalie Jordan Pickford sprang from his goal line with so much grace it defied all logic. Humans do not move like that, I thought. This was supernatural. With his hair slicked back *Peaky Blinders* style, Pickford lunged to his right. He stretched his entire body out and speared his right hand into the top corner of the goal. Miraculously, in his flight of desperation, he tipped Adarabioyo's header out of bounds with his fingertips. It would later be voted as the best save in the month of January in the EPL and then one of the best saves of the season.

The away end exploded in deafening song. I reared back and chanted right alongside the thousands of Scousers at a volume I didn't even know I could reach.

"Evvvvv . . . er . . . ton! Evvvvv . . . er . . . ton! Evvvvv . . . er . . . ton!"

It was primal and urgent.

The away end chant for Pickford was so thick and heavy I could feel it blow away all the bad spirits and ghosts of Everton's past that had been swirling around us.

Everton had life. Everton hadn't been relegated just yet.

Since there was no jumbotron to show a replay, our collective memories went into hyperdrive. Every couple of seconds, a different Everton supporter near me shook their head in disbelief and said something to call up and shape the memory of Pickford's save.

Pickford felt the juice, too. His back was to us and he waved his arms up and down, encouraging us to continue chanting.

"He's England's number one! He's England's number one!" the away end thundered, in honor of Pickford's status as England's national team's starting goalie.

I stared out at the gorgeous old stadium and this perfect night of football. Something ancient and warm and mystical flooded over me. Every true football supporter has a transcendent moment when they fall deeply in love with the game, a definitive mark in their life when they transition from being a passive bystander of the sport into someone who simply can't live without it. Sometimes this transition happens in a moment when there's a sudden flash of skill, a wonder strike from far outside the box that hits the back of the goal with a crack of thunder and the stands erupt in madness and a feeling rushes into a fan's heart in the rapturous manner of a first love. Sometimes it happens slowly over time, all the elements of the game revealing themselves quietly, the sights and sounds and tastes becoming the sweet dance of courtship, until one day you notice the elements of the game lingering with you well after you've left the football ground.

Mine was a blend of the two. From the moment of the save on, I knew that I never wanted to be without the beautiful game in my life. I would commit to it until the end of my days. I'd crossed a divide where the game of football went from something on the physical plane to something spiritual: a living entity inside me.

Suddenly, I understood the opening line of one of the best books about English football ever written, *Fever Pitch* by Nick Hornby: "It's in there all the time."

Until then, I'd been a fan. I'd *thought* I'd been a supporter, but I wasn't. I hadn't felt the sensations currently going through me at a molecular level: the symphony of song and chant and drumming; the hope in staying up and the full-throated and raw desperation and the demand that the boys fight to the end; a pitch so green that my heart knew it must look like this in heaven; the floodlights illuminating all our childhood dreams; the century-old stand that was a testament to the old ways of steel and timber and calloused men who toiled in the Industrial Revolution; the dark art of the cursing in the away end tickling the most devilish parts of my sense of humor; and the primitive comfort of belonging to a tribe.

The sport of English football was inside me now.

## CHAPTER ELEVEN

# Sugden Sports Centre, Manchester, February 6, 2024

From Liverpool, I took a train across the Scottish border to its picturesque capital city, Edinburgh. There, I met my twin sister, Becky. She and I live a mile apart in Minneapolis, where she works for the insurance and finance company Allianz. While not a huge football supporter, she had always longed to visit Edinburgh, and took this as her chance. It was lovely to share this part of the trip with her. Becky's presence was a boost of energy to me in my travel-weary state. We walked every inch of the city, going underground into an ancient pub and even further underground on a ghost tour that took us into the bowels of the city. There were quaint bookstores with cozy chairs nestled next to fireplaces, and surprisingly world-class food.

On a frigid night, we popped into a pub to get out of the rain and met an eighty-year-old Scottish troubadour named Roy. He referred to himself as "the Last True King of Scotland." He regaled me with endless stories about the good old days on the terraces of UK football, when they used to drink all day and piss into plastic bags and then launch the piss bags at the opposing supporters in the stands. He politely excused himself from our conversation and walked directly onto a tiny stage. The pub exploded with applause, and Roy belted out a rousing set of rebel ballads, thrashing on his guitar. When he stepped offstage, he came back over and returned to our conversation about UK football without skipping a beat.

Becky and I trained south back to England and arrived in Manchester, the last stop on the first leg of my journey. Tired as I was, and as much as I looked forward to getting home and eating home-cooked meals and sleeping in my own bed, being in this football-crazed city instantly energized me. Becky and I spent our days immersing ourselves in Mancunian football lore. We went to the Museum of English Football, shopped at Classic Football Kits, had coffee with the creator of Bands FC, a website that blends music and English football and makes badges and kits related to the musicians, and even ate dinner at the restaurant owned by Manchester City FC manager Pep Guardiola.

After Becky flew home, I traveled to Bury, a suburb north of Manchester so grimy it was as if black pudding became a municipality. When I came out of the Bury tram station, I saw an eleven-year-old boy vaping, blowing huge clouds of smoke that smelled like a chemical piña colada. I was chasing down a storyline involving Bury Football Club, a team in the ninth tier of English football that was known as a "Phoenix Club." It had died a few years ago due to financial mismanagement but was now rising from the ashes thanks to a group of lifelong, die-hard supporters banding together to bring the club back to life.

I spent the morning in a stinging rainstorm reading tombstones at the town cemetery surrounding Gigg Lane, Bury FC's home pitch, and talking to gravediggers. A day later, I attended a match at Gigg Lane. The pitch was so skunked and rotten that I felt like I was in a dog park. The hospitality of the Bury supporters in the club bar after the match was authentic and lively, a warm hug from the beauty that is non-league football. But the only game highlight came at halftime, when I saw a sign on a toilet stall labeling the stall as the official office of the much-maligned former owner of Bury Football Club.

After my recent conversion experience into a living and breathing football addict, it seemed being around people talking about football wasn't enough. Only one thing could reach the hard-to-get-to spot and scratch the itch: playing the game myself. So, I got in touch with Jack Bies, the Footy Addicts media manager and Manchester resident, and he invited me to the game he himself organized and played in. He described it as a high-level game, one that street ballers and a few ex-professionals were known to show up at, but he assured me the people were friendly and accommodating. I was desperate enough to be back on the field to take his word for it and give it a try.

At 6:30 a.m. on a brutally cold early February morning, I slunk through the dark, cramped side streets of southwest Manchester. I arrived at the Sugden Sports Centre underneath the A57 motorway in complete darkness. A huddle of hooded men were already there. We were junkies, all right.

Jack was among them. "It's so great to have you join us today," he said. He had immigrated from Poland and had an accent.

"Thanks so much for the invite, dude. It means a lot to me," I told him.

The caged field we gathered on was similar in almost every way to the first one I played on in West London: boards on the bottom, fence on the top, skunked turf, and graffiti splattered all across the underside of the motorway.

It felt like a scene in a *Rocky* montage. Sunrise started to creep over the horizon and sent a low tide of warm orange light across this cold and gray industrial city. It was still hard to believe that I was actually here, about to play the sport of football in one of England's best football cities.

As we warmed up, Jack played some music. He had already set the teams and he distributed the colored pinnies accordingly. He read out the rules and code of conduct; there would be no tolerance for bad behavior. Then he set his watch to mark the time that the goalies would be switched.

He blew the whistle and it was game on. Within seconds, I was in an all-out sprint for a ball in the corner with an opponent directly on my right hip. He was short and stocky and had a shaved head. He was wearing a vintage Manchester United kit and had a pinched grimace. We both arrived at the ball at the same time.

I felt the Mancunian slyly grab my right forearm and give it a little tug to try to knock me off balance. When that didn't work, he tried to hip check me into the sideboards. But I had already hunkered down low and got small so when he hit me, I caromed off the boards and all the energy went right back. In the slight separation that created, I won the ball and passed it cleanly to a teammate for a scoring chance.

As we ran up the pitch together, Jack slid up next to me. "Welcome to Manchester," he said, smiling.

The play at Sugden lived up to the hype. Everyone could absolutely ball out. Within a few minutes, I was gassed. But Jack was an easygoing leader and made me feel okay being the game's resident Dorf. This was a true reflection of Footy Addicts' mission: football was for everyone here, even a short, chubby bastard.

Jack was on the other end of the spectrum. In fact, he was one of the best players that I had ever played with. He was an absolute workhorse, fundamentally sound, with a nose for the ball like a striker's. Throughout the game he repeatedly saved my ass. I needed it, because the opposing team had a player who was not *one* of the best I'd ever played with but unequivocally the greatest streetball player I'd ever faced. I learned later that his name was Andrei Valimareanu and he was from Romania. He wore a Barcelona kit and had the long, thick beard of a Cuban revolutionary. He casually feasted on me for the entire hour. It wasn't a loud mauling but more of a subtle cleaning, like a hawk delicately picking the meat off the bone of a fresh kill, one piece at a time. When he called out to his teammates and directed traffic from his midfield position, his voice had the soft and tender yet soaring cadence of Robin Pecknold, the lead singer of Fleet Foxes.

When Andrei had the ball, which was all the time, I tried to defend him. I truly did. I manned up and jockeyed him all over the pitch. But he had huge, centaur-like haunches and he simply shooed me away like an annoying fly. Worse still, his feet moved like the hands of a pickpocket. He had a bag of tricks, these small shimmies and shakes and step overs. He put me in the spin cycle more than once, turning me around and around, sending me in whatever direction he wanted.

He was also a wonderful, humble guy to play with, though. After each of his many goals and assists, he simply smiled and gave out low fives to his teammates. No big celebration, no yelling.

After I miraculously stole the ball from him one time, he turned and said, "That was great defense." Then he gave me a low five. It felt like Christmas.

After one series where Andrei had me dancing like Richard Simmons and then scored a particularly nasty goal, Jack came over to let me in on a little secret. "Andrei is too humble to tell you, so I guess I will," Jack said, throwing an arm around Andrei. "This man is closing in on playing *five hundred* Footy Addict games."

"Holy shit, five hundred!" I said.

"It's just a number, my friend," Andrei said.

"Every game with a smile, too," I said.

"If you can't smile while you play, there is no point in playing, correct?"

The other player who most stood out to me on the opposing team was Yang. Unbelievably small, and to my eye in his late sixties, he wore thick gray sweatpants that draped off him and old, battered cleats that looked like slippers. But he had a first touch like Velcro: the ball stuck to his toes like I'd never seen before.

During the entire hour, I never saw him so much as jog. How, then, did he always appear in the exact right place at the exact right time? The entire game seemed to flow through him, the ball seemed always to find him, and there was an eternal elegance to his game, as if his playing style came from the moon and the tides. I stopped trying to defend him because the second I moved, Yang would disappear and reappear in a different spot, and all I was doing was chasing shadows.

After the game, Jack and Andrei and I stood together under

the motorway and talked. Early in my trip, I had met a Scotsman on a train who told me that the farther north I got from London, the nicer and cooler the people were going to be. Jack and Andrei seemed to prove the claim. It made me think of the Northern Soul movement in music, and I felt like we were doing something akin to that. During the late 1960s and early 1970s, a music and dance scene emerged in Northern England and the Midlands that combined elements of the British mod scene and Black American soul music. The music was an escape from punishing riots, recession, unemployment, mine closures, the rise of the far right, and football hooliganism. It was all about absorbing different cultures to create something new. Now, the pickup footy scene in Manchester was connecting a Polish immigrant, a Romanian immigrant, and an American idiot. We took our varied backgrounds and shared interests and created something new: a football friendship. Even though I had literally just met both men, it felt like I'd known them my whole life. We played together the next day. And after that, I asked them out on a man date.

"I'm coming back in a month and a half," I said. "Would you like to go to a Stockport County game with me?"

Jack and Andrei both smiled. We were all footy addicts, and I already knew their answer.

"Yes, of course," they said.

A few days later, I traveled home. On the flight, the plane's preset playlist called up the song "Closing Time" by Semisonic. I became a wee bit misty listening to the lyrics and hearing my friend John Munson's singing voice and sweet bass riff. After years of doubt and rejection, I'd actually moved forward, both in my life as a writer and as a football supporter. I'd put distance between myself and the darkness of relegation, popping my head out of the ground like a prairie dog. It felt great.

I'd spend some time at home, put in some work at the day job, and then get right back on the road in the UK. I had a second leg of the journey to complete. Bring it on, I thought.

# Second Leg of Trip

## CHAPTER TWELVE

# Minneapolis, Minnesota, and Arbroath, Scotland, March 21-26, 2024

For a month and a half, I worked at Hiawatha Supply during the day and wrote at night—the universal schedule of starving artists. On March 20, I flew from Minneapolis to London, arriving at Heathrow at dawn. I stood for a tedious forty-five minutes in the Customs queue, only to have my passport not scan in the reader. I was quickly escorted to an Immigration agent. I handed over my passport and he studied the photo. He paused and read his computer monitor. I assumed he had now been notified that I had recently been in the UK for more than a month. He turned to me and scanned my face with drill-bit eyes.

"What brings you *back* to England, Mr. Smith?" the agent asked from behind a Plexiglas divider. He was a thick chap with a serious high and tight haircut.

"I'm here to watch football," I said.

"Yeah?" he said perkily. He held my passport out and to the side, like a dog owner teasing his pet. "Who are you here to see?"

"Stockport County," I said, naming the better-known team among the ones I'd soon be visiting.

The agent instantly put my passport down and hammered a stamp onto it.

"Proper club," the agent said. "Welcome back to England."

I traveled by train to Edinburgh and, with only a minute to spare, transferred to another train that took me up along the rugged northeast coast of Scotland to Arbroath, a small port city. I was there to speak with Peter Clarke, the longtime groundskeeper at Gayfield Park. On a quick tour of the Gayfield Park pitch, Clarke bent down to inspect a mysterious item in the goal box.

"Lobster tail," he said, showing it to me before nonchalantly tossing it in the trash. "No big deal" was the message: this was normal here. Every day, the North Sea roared mere feet away from his immaculate pitch and delivered something that he had to contend with.

For the last nineteen years, Clarke has had the unique distinction of tending to the pitch that is closer to the North Sea than any other in the United Kingdom—a small service road is the only thing that separates the ground where Arbroath FC plays from the sea. It's a quirky distinction for a quirky team playing in a quirky little city dug hard into the shoreline two hours northeast of Edinburgh. The football team is nicknamed the Red Lichties for the colored lights that lead the fishing boats back to shore. The town has a nightclub dedicated to Danny DeVito. BBC Scotland made a short video about Arbroath FC titled *What If Wes Anderson Directed Football Games?*, which consisted of shots of a match day at Gayfield Park in a style mimicking that of the idiosyncratic filmmaker. I could now not un-see the Wes Anderson effect.

"We can have upwards of a hundred seagulls come here at night," Clarke said. "They come and lie on the grass and pick their old feathers out. In the morning the pitch is just white." To make matters worse, Clarke said another "big thing is seagull crap," and that the gulls also bring "crabs and bits and pieces off the beach. They leave all the scales. They leave all the guts and stuff on the pitch. It's a nightmare."

When I met him, Clarke was preparing the pitch for a critical match to take place the next day. In 2019, Arbroath FC had won promotion to the second-highest division of Scottish football, the Scottish Championship. They'd managed to stay there for the past five years, punching above their weight as the only part-time professional team in a league of full-time clubs. Whereas players on the other nine Championship clubs are paid to train and compete full-time, Arbroath FC players only train twice a week and spend the rest of their time working other jobs. Their run in the Championship looked like it might be coming to an end. If they lost their Saturday 3:00 p.m. game against Partick Thistle FC from Glasgow, relegation would be all but certain.

Clarke, like the players, is a part-timer for Arbroath FC. He is also the groundskeeper for the Arbroath Bowling Club and the Arbroath United Cricket Club, and he runs his own landscaping company. This means he spends just about every single day working outside in a part of Scotland known for having only two seasons: June and winter. Nevertheless, he's slogged on.

By all indications, he was doing an incredible job. The pitch was immaculate. I couldn't fathom how he'd achieved such a pristine green surface in a place where I was scratching my head to understand how anything grew at all. Wind gusted over the seawall and across the pitch. Beyond the wall, the notoriously moody North Sea was downright schizophrenic, changing its disposition every few minutes. It went from the serene maritime splendor of a seaside town with gently fluttering flags and the lazy rhythmic bobbing of sailboats and buoys to bombastic waves crashing on the rocks and spraying liquid shrapnel in the air to a sea sky so blue and pure that it possessed an ethereal quality, the towering clouds interspersed with shafts of golden sunlight that seemed to be leading me to Valhalla, and then immediately back to a blitz of cold, concussive winds so intense it scrambled my brain.

I watched Clarke put a final cut on the pitch with his small hand mower, moving back and forth in the beautiful symmetry of workmanlike fortitude and artistry, cutting the signature lines into the pitch for match day. When he was done, he came over to join me in the stadium terrace in the corner of the ground where I'd sought shelter.

"What is your secret?" I asked, my teeth chattering. "This pitch is amazing."

"Just hard work," Clarke said humbly. His face was raw and red.

"Nah, man. There's something more going on here. I can tell that this pitch gets some serious love. It seems to be a huge part of your life," I said. "Are you constantly thinking about it?"

"All the time," Clarke admitted. "It's always right there. I would go on holiday with my family and the pitch was the one thing I would be thinking about. If you go anywhere, go to another ground, you're always thinking, What are they doing here? What's happening there? I'm always thinking about how I can improve this or how I can improve that."

To grow and maintain a professional football pitch in normal conditions is a full-time job. Most professional football clubs employ an arsenal of groundskeepers who use state-of-the-art seeding and fertilizing practices. Others, like Tottenham, simply build a multimillion-dollar conveyor so they can move the field when it's not in use to a place where they can optimize the growing conditions. But out here on the margins of professional football, Clarke worked all his magic alone, in just twenty hours per week.

"The main challenges are the wind, the cold, and the salt," he told me, sounding affable and lighthearted about it all. "During the wintertime when the tide's high, the pitch tends to be quite wet under the ground. The water stays quite a long time, too. Then when the clocks change and the seasons change, all the water disappears. The ground becomes so dry. Like you see now, out there in the middle of the pitch." Clarke pointed to an imperfection that only he could see.

The bright sun poked out and it was glorious. Then, suddenly, it dipped behind a huge bank of clouds and the temperature plummeted again. A curtain of rain moved in and rinsed every single surface for a few minutes and then swept back out to sea. All the while, the wind howled. Both of us shivered.

"Besides the weather, what else affects your ability to manage the ground?" I asked.

"Well, a lack of budget is a big thing as well. There's not an awful lot of money to throw about and be able to do things that you really need to do on the ground."

"If you had the money, what would those things be?" I asked.

"A sprinkler system," Clarke said.

I couldn't believe he didn't have one already. "I have to take a hose out and just keep moving the hose about all day," he confirmed.

Mercifully, the sun poked out again for a prolonged time. It was revelatory, better than any sunshine I've ever felt. Clarke and I turned our heads skyward and took full advantage of the spotlight of relief for five minutes. Our bodies melted slow and steady like candles. Then the sun abruptly disappeared again, and I went back to being miserable.

"I was told that Bovril is the only thing that will help me during a Scottish football match," I said, referring to the piping hot beef tea beloved by Britain's cold-weather football supporters.

"Yes, a proper pie and a Bovril will get you straight," Clarke confirmed with a laugh.

I was feeling a bond with Clarke, of the kind that can form between people who perform similar jobs. When I come across another person who knows what it's like to suffer outside, I tend to feel a connection. I started telling him about my work in the landscaping industry in Minnesota, and before I knew it, I was talking about another job I'd had as a snowplow operator.

"I plowed snow for close to fifteen years. I drove a big plow truck and led a crew. Then I became a machine operator and drove a snow tractor." Without thinking twice about it, I admitted to him how that job had really felt. "It broke me," I confessed.

"Right," Clarke said. "Hard life, that."

"The worst part was that all my snow shifts were open-ended. For five months, I never knew when I was going to work or for how long. Every weather forecast filled me with anxiety that I could not shake off. After a while, I learned to absolutely despise snow. Even in the late summer, it could be dry and dusty and one hundred degrees and I was already worrying about winter."

"Well, you knew what was coming. That's the thing. You knew what was next after August and September," Clarke said sympathetically. "You knew what was behind October."

"Every single time it snowed, I had to go out there and deal with it," I said. "No matter the time or the conditions, I had to go out and deal with it. It broke something inside me."

"I had a similar thing happen to me," Clarke said.

"Really?" I asked. I was shocked. He seemed so jovial.

"Yeah, really similar," Clarke said. "Most people, if it is a horrible day here, they will think, Oh, you know what? It's a rubbish day, I'll come back tomorrow and I'll finish. But I couldn't do that here at Gayfield Park. I'd have to go out and work in the worst weather because we'd have a game on Saturday and the entire community was counting on it. So, I'd have to get the pitch ready for the team and the town. No matter the weather. I'd be out there walking the pitch, and it would be driving rain and there's nothing else I could do because it had to get done."

"Amen, brother."

"Even if I have the right gear on, the weather is still going to take it out of me. After a long day outside, working both jobs, I'd go home at night and I could not get warm. It would take hours—and I mean hours—for me to get warm. Just like you, it started to affect my mood, my relationships, and my holidays. I started to think, This isn't good. I started to really struggle with all this work."

He looked over at me and grinned. "This is my last season as groundskeeper here at Gayfield Park," he said. "I need a break from being out here." He shrugged, looking at the pitch. Then he stood up, yawned, stretched out his arms, and rotated his torso.

"Well, Todd from America, I've got to chalk the lines now," he said with a laugh. "Always more to do, and none of it is inside."

I returned to Gayfield Park for the match the next day. Clarke had told me that before Arbroath FC got promoted, they'd sometimes only get about three hundred fans at games, in a park that had a maximum capacity of 6,600. That wasn't the case at the moment. Though it wasn't exactly full, there were about two thousand people at the game. Not bad, given that that was nearly a tenth of the population of the town.

The vibe felt like a minor-league baseball game: fun, a little wacky, family-friendly, and with local pies and refreshments. There was a sign that pointed to "Food Kiosk Toilets" as if there was no separation between the three items. The merch store was a shipping container with a window cut into the end of it. There was a wall of bricks and plaques with names of Arbroath supporters such as Smudge, Stoosh, Smuth, Punks & Skins, Wee Terry, Cruickshanks, and one supporter simply known as The Hash. There was already a line for the legendary Pie Hut. There were old-school mods in fresh Doc Martens next to football wonks in Adidas Gazelles next to drunky trailer-park dwellers. It was sublime.

A gaggle of elderly Scotsmen who all looked like Alex Ferguson were huddled in a lower terrace just a few feet from the pitch. They wore tightly knitted Arbroath FC scarves and Arbroath hats with pins pressed into the cuff and long winter coats. They genuinely seemed arsed about everything. They took shots at Pep Guardiola and Newcastle and "all the bloody oil money in the game." Their banter flew around in shorthand, a language unto themselves filled with their own unique references. It was obvious to me that they had stood together in the place for games for years. They seemed burrowed into the section like bears in a hibernation den.

I stood close to them and watched the Partick Thistle goalkeepers practicing goal kicks. They'd take a few steps back, run to the ball, and strike it with all their might. The ball would take off into the air with promise. But then it would get hit by the mighty winds of Gayfield Park and abruptly fall to the ground, like a duck shot out of the sky. It was an exercise in futility that provided the Arbroath supporters tremendous amusement.

"There you go, boys," one of the men in the bear den said. "Our home field advantage." Everyone laughed and cheered.

Despite the monumental task ahead for Arbroath FC, hope was still alive among the supporters. That didn't surprise me, coming from a place with an illustrious history of steadfast belief in a bright, independent future. In my time in Arbroath, I'd visited the towering relic of the Arbroath Abbey, where the most famous document in Scottish history was composed. The Declaration of Arbroath was a letter to Pope John XXII written in 1320, most likely by the town's abbot, and signed by thirty-nine nobles, barons, and freemen. It was a formal defense setting out Scotland's case that it was an independent, sovereign kingdom. The letter's most famous lines are: "It is in truth not for glory, nor riches, nor honours that we are fighting, but for freedom—for that alone, which no honest man gives up but with life itself."

Every Arbroath supporter I talked to believed the team could stave off relegation. They gave me elaborate scenarios, a combination of stats and facts and miracles that the club just needed to do. This was the dark arithmetic of "Relegation Math."

When a club is in the relegation zone, its supporters will huddle together over pints at the pub or a kitchen table or anywhere, really, and craft narratives that include potential wins and losses and point totals needed to deliver them to safety. They obsess over their upcoming home matches and away matches and the strength and form of the opponents. It becomes a sort of bastardized version of *A Beautiful Mind*, with supporters performing mental gymnastics.

There is a quaint tradition in the lower leagues of Scottish football where the youngest supporters are put in charge of leading the chanting and drumming and singing. And at the Arbroath FC game, there were a great number of kids around. They were scampering about seemingly everywhere. A pack of ten of them walked back and forth on the terrace with a megaphone and drum, making a racket. With the dreadful form that began the match, I realized that the kids *had* to be the ones to lead the cheers because the adults were too busy stewing.

Partick Thistle scored in the fifteenth minute. After that, clouds rolled in and winds continued to pummel the ground and the game grew quite lifeless and miserable. The only thing left to do was get a pie and Bovril. I'm both proud and mortified to report that the Bovril delivered. Big-time. I was freezing, and it seemingly stitched me back together from being pulled apart all day with its piping hot temperature and rich body—it tasted like a slow-cooked pot roast, liquefied. I held on to that sweet little cup of beef tea with my entire being.

At the seventieth minute, the game entered its saddest stage.

Arbroath was feckless, and it was clear to everyone in attendance that this wasn't going to end well. They desperately needed the win, and they were not going to get it. The Relegation Math was finally and unmercifully against them.

Arbroath Football Club were going down.

I found Peter Clarke standing on the side of the terrace near the bear den of old-timers. He was mixed into the crowd, part supporter and part groundsman. Despite everything the North Sea had thrown his way, his pitch had held up and still looked beautiful.

"Hey, man," I said, sliding up next to him.

"There you are, Todd from America. How was the Bovril?"

"Life-changing."

"I bet. Nothing beats it."

"Quick question: How come there's no singing or chanting here?" I said. Other than the kids, and a man hammering away on a child's kazoo, I hadn't heard much noise from the supporters at all.

"Because we are shite," Clarke said, laughing.

Meanwhile, across the stadium, the three hundred Partick Thistle fans sequestered in the away supporters' cage were going nuts with song.

"So what happens now when Arbroath goes down?" I asked quietly.

Clarke took a second. He plotted out his response. It arrived in stages like a set of chores performed in exact order to complete the care for his beloved pitch.

"When the club goes down, they will lose hundreds of season ticket supporters. It might go back to the numbers we talked about earlier. Just three to four hundred people here. When the tickets aren't sold, the money goes down. When they don't have the money from the gate, they don't have the money to sign the players they need to get back up. Without the players it takes to win, the next thing to go are the points in the standings. When you lose the points, you are finally in that brutal spiral of the lower leagues," Clarke said bluntly.

"Jesus," I said jokingly. "That's the saddest shit I've ever heard. I might need another Bovril."

"Get me one, too," Clarke said, jostling my elbow.

But then Clarke did something that surprised me. He didn't rag on the club or the team or the players or the lack of money for a sprinkler system. He burned no bridges. Clarke stayed positive.

"In the 2022 season, we finished second in the league and almost went up to the Scottish Premiership. The top league. We got beat by Kilmarnock, down at Kilmarnock. In that game, we went one nil up, and all of us thought our dreams of making the Scottish Premiership were made," Clarke said. "They beat us two to one, and then we got beat in the playoffs to go up. But for a part-time team, that's an amazing thing to have seen."

"What a run," I said.

"We've been in the Championship League now for five years. That's the longest a part-time team has been in the Championship, so that says a lot on its own," Clarke said proudly. "To get relegated is a new beginning. It's a fresh start next year. There's a new manager in. So, now he gets to put his own take on the team. All the teams in the league below will be part-time clubs like Arbroath. So that makes a big difference as well."

"There's a more level playing field," I said. "There's more balance."

"Yeah. Roughly the same budget," Clarke said.

The game was in the dying seconds. Hundreds of Arbroath FC supporters milled around the terraces. Their dreams of staying up had finally died. But there was still good cheer about. Lots of backslapping and giving hugs. The kids kept singing and pounding their drums. The drunk kept blowing his kazoo.

Clarke held strong, too. For a man who had made his living out on this pitch, tending to the grass while being battered by the elements, the North Sea raining down lord knows what on him, his body suffering a level of cold that takes hours to shake off, he remained incredibly hopeful. He knows that the bad weather and the bad losses are only temporary. The storms always end eventually.

"Now the club has the chance to do something special," Clarke said, smiling. "It has the chance to get promoted. And that's everything for us. There's no feeling like it."

CHAPTER THIRTEEN

# Stroud and Nailsworth, Gloucestershire, March 27-30, 2024

From Arbroath, I traveled by train back to England and arrived in the pastoral countryside of the Cotswolds, an eight-hundred-square-mile area due west of London. From the top-floor window of my Airbnb in Stroud, I could see just how buttery soft life here was in spring. I stared hypnotically at gentle rolling hills that sprawled across the horizon like great waves of green velvet. Stone cottages dotted the landscape, tendrils of smoke rising from their chimneys. In the Creamsicle-colored sky, hundreds of small birds took flight and moved in a sweeping, synchronized aerial display. Down below on the cobblestone street, townsfolk wore Wellington boots and wax-coated Barbour jackets. They shopped at the farmer's market, carting their local craft cheeses and artisan breads and grass-fed meats around in wicker baskets.

After the brutal windscape of Scotland, this was a welcome reprieve. I spent a couple of days letting the Cotswolds unfold before me like a living fairy tale. I took a walk in the woods that brought me across a stone footbridge arching over a babbling stream. I puttered along narrow brick lanes where there always seemed to be a cafe tucked away with a sandwich board out front advertising tea and homemade scones and toasties in colorful chalk. I wandered by cottages made of honey-colored limestone with gray slate tile roofs and gardens busy with bright flowers and bumblebees. They sat on roads lined with dry-stacked stone walls that held in baaing sheep and enormous stately homes with royal lineage and Downton Abbey aesthetics led up to by crushed-pebble driveways that wound through immaculately tended grounds. Regardless of the forecast, there was always a chance of rain. But it was almost always gentle and refreshing and immediately followed by a parade of towering white clouds out of the opening credits to *The Simpsons*. My consistent impression was that this was a place of privilege, where life was comfortable. My other impression was that this was not a football town. It was like Bristol, if the graffitied urban jungle was replaced by pastures for grazing and antique Rolls-Royces.

That impression remained in Nailsworth, a small, idyllic village and the home of the football club I had come to watch, the Forest Green Rovers. A small creek bordered by ancient stone walls tumbled past a clock tower in the village center. I spotted at least one of seemingly every make of car that James Bond drove. There were banners in the village center that advertised meetings for the Nailsworth Flower Arrangement Society and a Bicycle Jumble. There were no banners for the Rovers. The only trace of their existence near the village center was an out-of-the-way road sign pointing up a steep hill to their stadium.

It likely didn't help that at the moment, they were bad. They were circling relegation out of League Two and back to non-league football, from whence they came. But as interesting as relegation always was to me, that's not why I was here. The team was unique on a number of other counts that I was curious to understand.

Their owner was Dale Vince, founder of the UK's largest green energy supplier, Ecotricity. He was just about the furthest thing from a typical capitalist entrepreneur. Formerly a New Age Traveler, his ethos was centered on leftist, anarchist, antiwar, and environmentalist causes, and he was known to participate in anti-government protests. With his company, he helped introduce solar energy, wind farms, and electric vehicles to the British mainstream. He also built a network of vehicle charging stations that stretched from the south of England all the way into Scotland.

His investment of millions of pounds into the Forest Green Rovers in 2010 initially seemed an odd choice. They were not a good or prominent club: for 121 years, they'd played non-league football. Furthermore, the team was so beset by financial problems that they'd resorted to placing ads in the *Financial Times* asking for donations to help cover the players' wages. But Vince came in and found a way to make sport and sustainability go hand in hand. In short order, they gained UN status as the first carbon neutral football club in the world. Bolt New Lawn Stadium is set up to run on 100 percent renewable energy through solar panels and windmill farms, and emissions from away matches are offset via carbon credits. The pitch is maintained organically, without chemicals or pesticides, using equipment like a robotic mower and tractor that run on biofuel. The pitch is also irrigated using recycled water—not only rainwater but filtered urine from the stadium toilets, through their "Pee to Pitch" initiative. The team kits are made from recycled plastics and coffee grounds. There are biodiverse gardens and beehives on the stadium grounds. And all the food is vegan. Even the players are required to eat vegan when they're on club premises.

This all very well might have been received by the British sporting public as a virtue-signaling circus if it weren't for the fact that the team got better, fast. In addition to replacing the greasy meat patties with spicy quinoa burgers, Vince and his staff replaced the stodgy old tactics the team had been using with those driven by advanced data analysis. The club hired Everton's head of academy recruitment, Richard Hughes, and quickly promoted him to director of football. Long before Hollywood came to Wrexham, and long before the use of *Moneyball*-style approaches had arrived at most lower-league teams, Forest Green Rovers were benefiting from star power, investment, and thoughtful recruitment and training methods in the Cotswolds.

Every season, there are hundreds of young players who are released from football academies due to a whole host of reasons: size, skill, speed, playing style, attitude, injury, coaching opinions, coaching changes, and personnel issues. This is the dirty and dark side of English football. The brutal fact is that 97 percent of the young players in the Premier League and professional academies never make the top squad. English football youth academy players are viewed as a disposable commodity—the chaff being separated from the wheat. But Hughes knew there was potential in these tossed-off players. Backed by statistical analysis, he began to target and recruit some of the broken toys who had washed out of Premier League and Championship academies and polish them up.

In the 2016–17 season, Forest Green Rovers broke out of

non-league football for the first time in their history and won promotion to League Two. Two seasons later, they made an epic run and finished in fifth place in the league, a huge accomplishment for such a small club. Two seasons after that, in 2021–22, they shocked the world of English football by winning the League Two title and being promoted as champions into League One.

But the good times were not to last. Days later, their talented young coach left for a Championship League club. In League One, Forest Green Rovers won their initial match versus Bristol Rovers, then lost all but five more games the rest of the season, fired their new coach, lost their captain and leading scorer to an ACL tear, and got relegated back to League Two. The next coach was Duncan Ferguson (aka "Duncan Disorderly"), whose fiery temperament and hard-man bravado were an odd fit from the start. Even the press release photo looked out of sorts. Vince was dressed in his typical hipster pirate flair—loose and billowy scarf and fingerless knitted gloves that showcased his painted fingernails—shaking hands with Ferguson, whose playing style had resembled a Scottish Highland Charge, with him running as hard as he could into the opposition. Ferguson won a single match out of eighteen he coached and subsequently left his coaching role after just a few months. Hughes, the mastermind behind so much of the club's success, left for another team. Forest Green then finished dead last in League One, and by the time I arrived, they were on the cusp of being relegated out of League Two and back to non-league football. They'd nearly completed the circle, though it wasn't of the sustainable, stable type I imagine Vince—or the fans—would have wanted.

I thought I would find a supporter base in Nailsworth and

Stroud who had been exhilarated by the rise and now held passionate opinions about how they could reverse the skid and get back on the right track. I'd misjudged. In the cushy Cotswolds, even this wildly interesting, odd, unique team was an afterthought. Life would be good when Forest Green Rovers were good. Life would still be good when they were bad.

The vibe on the ground on the Friday game day felt very much like a picnic in the park with a side game of footy. Bolt New Lawn Stadium was set at the top of the hill, with rolling green fields all around. The sky was painted bright blue and filled with puffy white clouds. People ate their vegan scrambles and drank their local beer. There was live music, but it was unrelated to the team: there wasn't any chanting or singing from supporters.

Inside the stadium I ran into Dale Vince in the posh Black and White hospitality lounge. He was dressed in chic camo pants and Balenciaga sock shoes and his trademark billowy scarf. I didn't spend much time with him, but he was a welcoming host, warm and kind. After walking past the wall where a quote from Albert Einstein was inscribed—"Nothing will benefit human health and increase chances for survival of life on Earth as much as the evolution to a vegetarian diet"—I took my seat in the main stand. The sky cycled from bright sunshine to tumbling clouds to quick bursts of rain and back to sunshine. Everything here was perfect except for the play on the pitch.

The Rovers were playing Stockport County FC, from Greater Manchester. Stockport was on the other end of the league table, eyeing promotion to League One instead of relegation to non-league football. Stockport was also the next stop on my itinerary, so I was eager to see them play. County were an absolute revelation.

The Rovers were an embarrassment from the start. For minutes on end, they did not even touch the ball. Then in the eighteenth minute, Stockport's Callum Camps unleashed a wonder strike from well outside the goal box that erupted like the popped cork of a champagne bottle into the Rovers goal. Though it was only 1–0 and early in the tilt, it was clear to everyone that this was the end. The twelve hundred away supporters were jubilant; the smaller number of locals didn't seem much bothered.

I had experienced a similar kind of blasé feeling in Bristol and at Fulham's Craven Cottage. My pet theory was that the cushy lifestyles of the average people in these pockets of wealth contributed to the general apathy of their football supporters. Day-to-day existence in these enclaves seemed to be too good to let the whims of eleven men in kits and cleats bother ruining it. In the urban gristle of the forgotten factory towns in the Midlands and in the north, however, where the weather was shit and work could grind a person down into anonymous oblivion, the football supporters were desperate for small glimpses of success and recognition. Often, their football clubs were the only things that stood a chance of offering that to them. That's why they gave everything they had to their clubs.

After ten minutes of daydreaming, my attention snapped back to the game when County struck again. Paddy Madden, their captain, took the ball in the midfield, and just before he was clattered into by two Rovers defenders, he laid it off perfectly to his teammate Ibou Touray, who was streaking down the left flank. Touray broke past a defender, raced to the touchline, and then suddenly crossed the ball into the box right on the turf, where Rico Richards one-timed it into the goal from the six-yard box. It was such an easy goal that it looked like County was running drills and the Forest Green players were the high-visibility orange cones.

Stockport notched one more goal early in the second half and won 3–0, a walk in the park. They had now gone seven games without losing: three wins and four draws. For the first time in fourteen years, they were on the brink of promotion. The Rovers, however, were going down for sure, and who knew if or when they'd ever be back up in the English Football League.

On my way out of the stadium, I stopped into a bar where I'd heard the most loyal Forest Green Rovers supporters spent their time to see if I could get a sense and feel of what a double relegation looked like. There were dozens of supporters but no animation or drowning of sorrows; no shouty calls for a new manager or bombastic screeds about the team's tactics; no vitriol about the players and their lack of quality or lamenting of missed opportunities; no groups huddled together and wielding relegation math. These Forest Green Rovers supporters knew their Quorn was cooked.

Thinking of the Albert Einstein quote on the wall, I remembered a quote from another famous thinker of the mid twentieth century. Elie Wiesel wrote, "The opposite of love is not hate, it's indifference."

That's exactly what this back-to-back relegation in the Cotswolds felt like. It wasn't love or hate. It wasn't hope or loss. It was simply indifference.

## CHAPTER FOURTEEN

# Stockport, Greater Manchester, April 1, 2024

I stood in the Ye Old Vic, a pub in Stockport that dated back to 1864, looking for a man named Dave.

Dave Marchbank was the chairman of the Stockport County Supporters Co-Op and a machine operator at a pharmaceutical factory. He'd invited me here to meet up before the game against AFC Wimbledon. On the way from the pub to the stadium Dave and I planned to meet up with my friends from the Footy Addicts, Jack Bries and Andrei Valimareanu, who had traveled here from nearby Manchester.

But there was a slight problem, one I'd run into before on my journey. I had no idea what Dave looked like. The description I was given of him—"sixties, looks like the sort of bloke that loves real cask ale"—fit every single man around me. I scanned the place, which had a real regulars-only, lived-in feel. Used books sat on the shelves. Coats hung on wood racks and umbrellas sat in the bin beneath. There was even a schedule set for the regulars to help with the pub's daily repairs and maintenance. The men's names were written on time cards that were placed in holders near an antique clock. Behind the wooden bar were beer engine sparklers, a sort of showerhead on the end of the tap that aerates and builds a nice frothy head on the pints they serve. The maker's website said that beer poured without a sparkler was strictly served for "Southern Pansies." The place was known for priding itself on the quality of its ales, especially cask ales, which are an unpasteurized, unfiltered, and naturally conditioned beer with a long history in England.

"Excuse me, sir, but are you Dave?" I asked a man standing alone at the bar. "Do I luk like a *fecking* Dave?" he said. He clearly had an Irish accent. This was not my guy. But something came over me, and it turned out to be the right call.

"You do!" I responded. "In fact, every man in here looks like a *fucking* Dave."

He clearly liked the way I'd matched his salty language. He tipped up the brim of his chappy cap and said, "Fair play. But I'm not Dave. Good luck finding yer man."

I wandered into a room in the back with a fireplace. Both sides of the room had large groups of Daves in Stockport County kits. They were huddled tightly together, and it seemed a wee bit suspect, like they were conspiring about something. Only a fool would interrupt these meetings, I thought. At the back of the room was a swinging door that led to the loo. Above it was a sign that read "To Surgery."

Giving up, I took my phone out, dug through my emails, and found a phone number.

"This is Dave," said the man on the other line. "Is this Todd from America?"

"Yes!" I said. "I'm at the Vic."

"Are you now? Me too. I'm in the small room at the back. By the fireplace."

A stout man with a glossy bald head stood up. His back was turned to me, but I could see the phone at his ear. When he turned my way, we both stood there, idiotically holding on to our phones, like it was a meet-cute in a romantic comedy. Which, in a way, it was. In our version, it was just two middle-aged men looking to share their love of football together. We hung up the call and shook hands.

"Welcome to Stockport, mate," Dave said, full of cheer and clapping me on the back. "Glad you made it."

"Me, too," I said.

Then he stepped aside and pushed out an arm in a sweeping motion and revealed what was behind him like a game show host announcing what I had won behind a curtain. Six Stockport County supporters were smiling at me.

"Lads, meet Todd from America," Dave said.

Each man stood up and introduced himself and shook my hand and welcomed me into their little corner of their pub in their little corner of the world. All the men scooted down the bench-style seating so I could squeeze in. Within moments I was made to feel that Stockport was home.

The men peppered me with questions, wanting to hear all about my trip. I nestled into the hot seat and spun my yarns about Grimsby and the Wolves away end and going on the road with the Everton Scousers and Pickford's save. One of the most important lessons in storytelling, though, is knowing when to end it. Get in, spin the tale, hit your marks, and get out. So before I overstayed my storytelling welcome, I steered the talk toward Stockport County FC and their season of dreams. County were currently at the top of the table in League Two, one point above both Wrexham and

Mansfield Town. Early in the season, they'd gone on a twelve-game winning streak, equaling a record for their current tier of football. There were only six games left in the season. If Stockport could keep up the kind of play I'd seen against the Rovers in Nailsworth, they'd be promoted.

"Let's talk about how Stockport County went on a twelve-game heater," I said to the guys. Laughter at my American sports vernacular rippled along the L-shaped pews like an EKG blip. "Wrexham and all their star power are still right on your heels at the top of the table. How do you feel?"

"We want promotion," Dave said proudly. All the men nodded their heads in unison. But no one else said a word.

This was a beleaguered fan base. These County supporters had seen the rise and fall and rise and fall of their beloved club for decades now, and they didn't want to say too much. Yes, County had a great chance to win the league and promotion. But things were never certain until they happened. This was a fan base that intimately knew the darkness that comes with relegation and the loss of hope. I could tell the lads didn't want to go there. So I didn't press the issue.

Instead, as the guys drank one more round of real cask ale and I drank my Coke, Dave stepped in and told a story of his own.

"It wasn't until my dad brought me to my first County game that I really fell in love with football," Dave said. "I was a young teenager and seeking some independence. I chewed my dad's ear one Saturday in the car and asked him to take me and my friend Andy to a Stockport game. My dad, Reg, turned round and said, 'Stockport play their matches on Friday evenings. Next time they are at home I will take both of you, drop you off, and pick you up after the game, how's that?' I didn't need to ask Dad twice.

"Dad stuck to his promise," Dave continued. "He took me and Andy to our first County match. County was playing Brentford on a Friday evening. Under the floodlights. The atmosphere and the cheering from the County faithful in the Cheadle End was on another level."

Dave and his dad began going to games together. They did this for decades. "Friday nights were County nights. Dad and I loved every minute," Dave said. "These were amongst the happiest times of my life. Football and dad and lad time and going to the pub for a few pints. Life was good."

But after Christine, Dave's mum and Reg's wife, was diagnosed with dementia, Reg stopped attending matches, seeing it as his duty to stay behind and care for her.

In 2019, Stockport County were on the brink of securing their first league title in fifty-two years and being promoted to the National League. County's away match against Nuneton was shaping up to be a historic day. Dave desperately wanted to take his dad to the match; they had waited so long for this moment. After much negotiation, Dave and his wife finally convinced Reg it was okay for him to leave the house just for this one day and go. But they'd waited too long—the match was sold out. Except for one ticket: a wheelchair seat, which came with a free pass for a caretaker. Before he could overthink it, Dave bought it.

Now there was an even bigger problem: How to get Reg Marchbank, a stubborn northerner, a former Mancunian sandblaster by trade, into a wheelchair. Dave and his wife secretly put a wheelchair in the boot of Dave's car. The morning of the match arrived, and Dave picked up his dad. They headed to the ground and arrived reasonably early. Dave managed to park the car quite close to the ground. Now it was finally time for the surprise. Dave nervously walked around the car. He popped open the boot and got the wheelchair out.

Reg saw it and made a stink face. "What's this, then?"

Dave explained the situation. "Dad, if you won't sit in it, we won't get to see the game," he said.

"Now you've done it, haven't you," Reg said. But eventually, reluctantly, he sat down in the wheelchair. He fussed until they saw they had excellent seats. Stockport County were crowned Champions of the National League North that day. Reg and Dave sat together in the disabled box with tears in their eyes.

Reginald Marchbank died on June 22, 2023. His body was cremated. Dave approached Stockport County and asked if his dad's ashes could be laid to rest in Edgeley Park, their historic ground. The management said yes, of course. The head groundsman dug a very neat square hole behind the goal that was directly in front of the Cheadle End. When Dave released Reg's ashes into the hole, he privately asked Reg to watch over the Stockport County players when they played, as he was now closer to the players than any of the lads in the Cheadle End Stand.

"My dad couldn't have responded better than overseeing Stockport's current form and possible promotion back to League One," Dave said.

"Here, here," said the guys.

This time the toast signaled our exit. Kickoff was approaching, and the pub was emptying. A steady stream of blokes poured out the front door. Just before I left the pub, I saw the Irishman standing in his same position at the bar. He gave me a nod. I nodded back. Both of us knew that I had entered the Vic as a stranger. Now there I was, part of a brotherhood of football supporters on our way to a match.

We marched in the streets of Stockport to Edgeley Park. Like the team, the city had recently rebounded from ignominious places. In 1844, the philosopher Friedrich Engels wrote that Stockport was "one of the dustiest, smokiest holes" of industrializing England. He was appalled by working conditions in the town, having witnessed thousands of workers living in squalor, covered with soot and grime, along the banks of the Mersey River. In 2003, *The Idler Book of Crap Towns* didn't take a much rosier view of Stockport, naming it one of the worst places to live in the UK. The authors wrote that anyone walking Stockport's streets should look out for "a shower of gob, McDonald's fries, and stones from the gangs of youths above," and that what amounted to entertainment in the city included "avoiding being stabbed on the infamous 192 bus and avoiding leaving your house as much as possible."

The turnaround had been remarkable. In 2023, Stockport was named one of the best places to live in England by *The Sunday Times* because of its quality schools, affordable housing, broadband speeds, access to parkland, and the health of its high streets. The city center was transformed by a one-billion-pound regeneration project, including improvements to the public transportation system. Its music and arts scene was burgeoning, along with its food and drink scene, to the point Stockport started being referred to as a "New Berlin."

To my eye, Stockport showcased a perfect blend of industrial past and vibrant present. I saw gorgeously preserved architecture such as the indoor central market and the White Lion Coaching House, a pub opened in the fifteenth century. Directly across the street from the White Lion was a mural that featured the iconic cover of Joy Division's album *Unknown Pleasures*, which was recorded in Stockport at Strawberry Studios. (Paul McCartney, the Stone Roses, and 10cc have recorded albums there, too.) I also saw a kickass independent shop called SK1 Records on a perfectly named street called "Little Underbank," where there was a sign telling me about the area's infamous history as home to ale houses of ill repute, one of which was called the Dust Hole.

The Dust Hole closed in 1896, thirteen years after Stockport County FC was founded. The club was voted into the Football League in 1905, the same year as Chelsea. Like all clubs, they had their ups and downs over the decades, but they always managed to stay in the English Football League. Until 2011. Poor ownership and management had resulted in the club suffering two consecutive years of relegation, dropping them into the National League. In 2013, they were relegated *again*, falling all the way to the National League North, in the sixth tier of English football. In 2014, no longer financially able to meet the demands of a full-time football club, County were forced into the brutal situation of being a part-time club. Players were reduced to practicing on Astroturf fields next to youth teams and pub-league donkeys, while working as lorry drivers and teachers and laborers to support themselves.

Dave and the lads I walked with to Edgeley Park remembered what it was like to wander through the wilderness of non-league play. "Years ago, I went to Hartlepool," Dave recalled, naming a club in the urban armpit of the northeast. "The weather was cold, with a strong swirling wind. Shortly after kickoff, the heavens opened and it didn't stop raining heavily for the rest of the game. The County supporters were housed in an open-ended terrace behind the goal, with absolutely no cover or shelter whatsoever. How and why I endured it, I'm not at all sure, particularly as we got beat six to nil."

Then, not so dissimilarly from Wrexham and Forest Green Rovers, a wealthy, committed new owner came in and changed things up. Mark Stott, a Manchester real estate magnate, bought Stockport County FC in 2020. The club was a skeleton, physically, financially, and spiritually. It needed the bones of infrastructure, the muscles of quality players, the brains of top-flight analytics. And it needed to find its soul again.

First, Stott hired Simon Wilson—an expert in analytics in team building—away from Manchester City.

Then Stott and Wilson hired Dave Challinor, a former Stockport center-half battle-axe and team captain, to coach the non-league roster into dogs of war.

In accordance with Wilson's principles, Challinor began building a Stockport County squad that was more similar in style to Liverpool's relentless attack than the possession-based system deployed by Manchester City. While Man City kills their opponents by controlling ball possession with a staggering number of short passes—death by a thousand tiny paper cuts—Liverpool slices their opponent wide open with a katana. Stockport prefers to do the same. They press high and play on the front foot. If they lose the ball, they try to win it back as soon as possible to spring forward with another attack. That was exactly what I had seen when

I watched them play the Forest Green Rovers the week before. The County players were quick to the ball, heavy on the tackles, and seemingly always on the attack.

At the same time, Stott asked Stockport County's president, Steve Bellis, who had worked for the club for more than forty years, to find a way to bring the team's soul back. Bellis did so in a grassroots, door-to-door type of way. He went to schools and youth football programs and convinced the young people of the town that supporting a local club is just as meaningful as supporting a big one.

"Mark Stott hasn't just invested in the football side of the club, he's done a tremendous amount of work with the community trust, who do great work across the whole town, especially for disadvantaged, underprivileged, and disabled people," Dave said. "Stockport is a county borough made up of a mixture of desirable and affluent areas, such as Bramhall and Cheadle Hulme, and also areas of some economic hardship, such as Brinnington and, indeed, Edgeley. This is one of the reasons that the football club is so important to Edgeley, as it attracts very much needed revenue, and it's one of the reasons the redevelopment of Edgeley Park would be so welcome."

In the 2021–22 season, County won promotion back to League Two in front of ten thousand home supporters. After eleven years of exile, they were back in the English Football League. The next year, they had a chance to get promoted again. It all came down to one game, which they led for nearly the entire match, then lost in a penalty shoot-out. After the match, Collinor refused to let the club, and the community, hang their heads. Instead, he put up a picture in the training ground of what their locker room had looked like after the loss, using it as motivation. He was saying that despite the gutting near miss, Stockport County were still on the right course. The players felt it. Dave and the supporters felt it, too.

As the lads and I kept marching to Edgeley Park, we linked up with my friends Jack and Andrei. They were welcomed right into the group, the good vibes from the pub still carrying along with us on the streets. It seemed that a similar thing was happening on every street corner: friends and family members were meeting up. Our pack merged with hundreds of other supporters who were streaming toward the match. Promotion was palpable. The sunlight hit differently. The sheet metal–gray morning sky gave way to a crisp blue that was a deeper shade than normal, like the glacial blue seen in icebergs. The songs and chants in the streets were playful and rowdy and full of hope and history and promise.

I suddenly became emotional. Though there were other matches I hoped to see in person, on the last stop of my trip, they would be played in a small, self-contained Scottish league. This was the last game I'd go to where the stakes were high. Indeed, in my whole two and a half months of traveling in the UK, they hadn't yet been this high. After so much relegation in my personal and professional life, I had finally arrived at a place on the cusp of promotion. I wanted promotion for Stockport and its football club, for Dave, for Reg, and for the lads I'd met at the Vic. I wanted promotion as a football supporter and as a worker and as a writer. I wanted to hear it and see it and feel it, badly.

We reached Edgeley Park and pushed through the turnstile, hoping that we had left all our losing behind us.

I stared into the mighty Cheadle End, a towering bank of seats for the most vocal of Stockport County home supporters. Fifteen minutes from kickoff this mass of humanity was singing and drumming in unison.

County started the same lineup as the one that had won decisively in Nailsworth. But they started off on the wrong foot. In the game's opening minutes, they botched passes and tackles all over the field. Soon, the four stands at Edgeley Park seemed to contract, squeezing and shrinking in anxiety. After a perfectly executed corner kick set piece was badly muffed by the usually infallible captain, Paddy Madden, the mood darkened even more.

County's sloppy play led to a well-positioned AFC Wimbledon throw-in, which reached all the way into County's six-yard box. An AFC Wimbledon forward corralled the ball and was clumsily run over from behind by County defender Fraser Horsfall (an appropriate last name for this incident), resulting in a penalty. Edgeley Park was now as cold and quiet as a morgue.

James Tilley, AFC Wimbledon's penalty shooter, got set to take the shot, staring straight into the Cheadle End. The County goalkeeper guessed completely wrong, and after diving in the opposite direction to the ball, he flopped like a fish out of water. But Tilley shanked it wide right. The entire Cheadle End sighed in relief.

At halftime, the score still 0–0, the announcer read something else I got a kick out of. "Stockport County would like to give a warm welcome to Jack and Andrei from Manchester and Todd from America! We hope you enjoy your day at Edgeley Park!" A small round of applause rippled through the crowd. I now knew why Dave had told us to keep our ears open at halftime.

The second half brought more cause to fear that this was not going to be County's day. Wimbledon put pressure all over County and had multiple scoring chances: an uncontested header off a corner kick clanked the bar, and a long-distance shot screamed wide by mere inches.

Those old demons of relegation had slunk out of the darkness and nibbled at the hope that County had been basking in all season. Maybe all of this was too much for this town and small club to bear, I thought. Maybe this was simply too much pressure. Maybe there was simply too much fear to overcome. Maybe the wounds from their relegations were, in fact, fatal. Maybe the hole that had been dug for decades from all their losing was actually their grave.

Despite the recent revitalization of the town and the football club, maybe they were destined to live in the shadow of Manchester United and Manchester City forever. Maybe all those sneering Mancunians in their jackets zipped up to the top and their cool haircuts and Adidas trainers had it right all along: "That Stockport is shit, innit."

Then, near the seventieth minute, County left back Ibou Touray burst through the darkness that had enveloped Edgeley Park and seemingly all of Stockport. He came screaming down the left wing with the ball and crossed it with the tenderness of a brushstroke. All our hopes and dreams spun in the air in gentle circles. The Stockport center forward rose above everyone and headed the ball at AFC Wimbledon's goal.

This was the moment that every County fan had dreamed of. This was the moment that would save them.

And the header missed the goal by inches. Five thousand County supporters screamed at once.

But something marvelous and inexplicable happened after the miss. There was a seismic shift in the Cheadle End. I could feel it in my feet. In the immediate aftermath of the blown header, the stand began to shake. The supporters were climbing out from under the rubble and beginning to cheer again. Energy and applause and positivity were coming through in waves of sound that radiated out in all directions and did not stop until the entirety of Edgeley Park was flooded with hope.

A few minutes later, County went on the attack. They began to press and press and press, desperate to score. This was the exact moment when Dave Challinor went for the kill. He made a tactical adjustment and moved the speedy Touray to the right side and then substituted in an offensively gifted player named Odin Bailey to line up on the right flank in front of Touray in the hopes their combined speed and skill would overwhelm a fading AFC Wimbledon back line.

The gods approved. Bailey took a pass from Touray on the right side of the pitch, deep in offensive territory. This was his sweet spot. He took off in a sprint with the ball, crossing right to left, waiting for the perfect moment to shoot.

Then it happened.

When he reached the top of the goal box, he took a few stutter steps and lasered a left-footed shot that screamed inside the back of the goal!

It was as though Edgeley Park had taken an epinephrine needle to the heart, like Uma Thurman's character in *Pulp Fiction*. The Cheadle End exploded in celebration. It was raw and unhinged bedlam. There were no more rows of seats or aisles. Just absolute limbs. It was a mass of bodies spilling everywhere. Arms and legs were swinging and flailing and flying in every direction. My body was launched all over in a celebratory swarm. I hugged my friends and high-fived strangers and hugged strangers and high-fived my friends. The stand was physically shaking from all the jumping and shouting and cursing and cheering. At the final whistle, the drumming became even more thunderous, and I was once again engulfed in a delirious mob.

This was what promotion sounded like. This was what promotion looked like.

After the game, I joined back up with Dave and the lads. We floated to another pub, walking underneath the world-famous Stockport Viaduct, which spans the Mersey River and delivers trains to and from Manchester. Built in 1839 with an estimated 11 million bricks, it was a major feat of engineering.

We wound our way past the new bus terminal and a historic Art Deco building called the Plaza Theatre and arrived at the Magnet Free House. The Magnet was built in 1840 and was formerly a coaching inn, where travelers could rest for the night. Now it was the perfect place for a celebratory pint. We commandeered a long wooden table in a former large living room and sat around it like we were at a royal feast.

In place of the desperation of relegation math was the confidence of promotion calculation. "We are at the top of the league. There are six games left. We have a game in hand over both Wrexham and Mansfield. We need just six points from those remaining six games. We are in great shape," Dave said smartly. "We have a clear way forward. Six points. That's what we need. We want to win the league. We want automatic promotion. We want to go up as Champions of League Two."

After an hour of revelry, we started to wind down. Dave and the lads had to go back to their regular lives outside of football, back to their spouses, kids, and responsibilities. But nobody seemed eager to leave such good feelings behind.

"One more round?" one of the lads asked.

Everyone at the table checked their phone for the time.

"Why not!" came the collective reply.

Dave took his glasses off and wiped his eyes. His face was rosy from the wind and the cask ale and the feeling of triumph. He had been waiting for this moment for so long. He had been waiting so long for a County season like this when everything clicked together, when the club could maintain the momentum, when the team formation jelled, when the substitutions were made at the right time, when the squad was deep and healthy, when the game tactics worked, and when the analytics were on point. He had been waiting for a season when the wins and the draws gave his club, his beloved club, enough points to help them rise out of the darkness, to climb out of this life of relegation, and they could stand for once outside the shadow of Manchester. When Stockport, the team and the town, would both matter at the same time again.

Looking at him, I thought about his father. The story of Dave and Reg Marchbank told me everything I needed to know about English football, which was coincidentally everything I needed to know about life in general. From the ashes of loss grows life, and if there's life there's a chance that hope will sprout, and if hope sprouts then the courage to keep fighting can build in your heart, and if there's courage in your heart there is room for dreams, and if you give yourself the space to dream there is always a chance that you can go on to do the impossible.

You can rise.

This was the exact feeling that I had set out to find.

This was what promotion felt like.

Promotion was in one more round before we parted ways. It was in the men pounding those pints like heroes.

Promotion was outside on the street as we collectively staggered to the train station and our Uber pickups with County's win soaked into our hearts so that we would never forget the match as long as we lived.

Promotion was walking on a bridge overlooking the mighty Stockport Viaduct, the very symbol of the industrial might of this town and this region of the country. Promotion was in one of the lads being joyously buzzed and stopping all of us for a moment and pointing at the Viaduct and announcing, "That bridge was made with a fuck-off amount of bricks."

Promotion was in the roar of laughter from this group of friends, the ones who had suffered together for so long out there in the wilderness of the lower leagues of English football and in life, because tonight was finally a celebration for their beloved club and their survival in this cold, hard place where they come from.

CHAPTER FIFTEEN

# The Isle of Lewis and Harris, Outer Hebrides, Scotland, April 5–8, 2024

On April 2, I landed in Inverness, Scotland. At dawn the next day, I got on a bus to the tiny port town of Ullapool. The drive went through one of the most remote corners of the Scottish Highlands, a journey into a mystical landscape of towering snow-capped mountains cloaked in the mist of ancient folklore. I could see how this might indeed be the land of giants and trolls and unicorns (the last of those being the official animal of Scotland).

Ullapool was only a stopover, though. I spent one night there at a combination bunkhouse, cafe, restaurant, bookstore, and music venue. According to their website, the Ceilidh Place was located "at the end of the A835 and the centre of the universe." In the bookstore, I stumbled upon a single copy of the novel *Romantic Comedy* by Curtis Sittenfeld. Not only a bestselling author, Curtis was also a fellow Minneapolis resident. I had met her at a summer party for writers and she was an absolute delight: funny and wicked smart and extremely humble. I took seeing her book here, three thousand miles from our hometown, as a sign. Books can come from any place and be written by anyone. Why not a mom like Curtis who wrote fiction in the morning and then ran errands at Target before she drove to pick up her kids at school? Why not a manure-slinging landscaper from Minneapolis? It gave me a renewed sense of purpose here, going into the very last part of my trip. I felt excited to keep pushing forward into territories unknown, and confident that someone like me could, in fact, travel this far and write about the thing I loved best, if I was brave enough to try.

The day after that, I boarded a massive Caledonian MacBrayne ship and sailed two and a half hours across the sea to the Isle of Lewis and Harris, the largest island in Scotland and third largest of the British Isles, after Great Britain and Ireland. Though it's big, it feels remote, and the total population is barely above twenty thousand. The island is one landmass but divided into two parts, and the inhabitants treat them as if they were two separate isles. Lewis takes up the northern two-thirds, and Harris the southern third.

I rented a cabin in the hinterlands, near a village named Leurbost that wasn't a village at all but simply a petrol station six miles south of Lewis's biggest settlement, Stornoway. I boarded a public bus at the port, and it took me out into a barren landscape. There were very few settlements and houses out here in the wilds, and I was worried I'd miss my stop because there seemed to be no stops.

"Hello, I'm Todd from America," I said to the bus driver. "I'm staying at the Heather Isle chalet."

"Aye," the bus driver said. "That's Don's place. Good lad."

"Can you tell me when to get off?"

"Aye."

A few minutes later, the bus driver pulled over in the middle of nowhere. There wasn't an actual bus stop in sight. Across the street to my left were two cabins side by side. Across the street from the cabins was the skeleton of an ancient house. Around it grazed a flock of sheep. The old house did not have a roof, and the remains of its walls stuck out of the turf like the bones of a prehistoric beast. I wondered what could have done that kind of damage to a structure. It looked like it had been battered by more than just time.

"Todd from America, this is your stop," the bus driver said.

An hour later, I heard the sound of car wheels on the gravel driveway of my cabin. Gordon Greenhowe, a native Lewis islander and vice president of Lochs Football Club, and his ten-year-old son, Ollie, were here to collect me. They had kindly offered to be my guides for the next few days to the Lewis and Harris Football League, helping to show me what football looked like in the strange and extreme landscape of the Outer Hebrides.

Despite what felt to me like cold weather—high thirties and low forties—Gordon wore shorts and a hooded sweatshirt. I wore many layers. It was a Friday, so there weren't any games scheduled to be played, but Gordon and Ollie took me on a tour of some of the pitches of the teams that made up the league.

We drove to the Point Football Club pitch, where we hoped to see a game played on Saturday. The winds coming off the sea were between 50 and 70 mph and deafening. They slashed across my body as I got out of the car, tearing at my clothes, at my limbs, and at my mind, driving away every clear thought and leaving behind a primal madness.

A storm had moved in at terrifying speed and began to assault the island. It was named Kathleen. There were reports of the sea launching boulders into the lower roads. All passenger boats had been docked. All shipments of food and provisions were canceled. All flights had been canceled. The grocery stores were filled with islanders gathering life's necessities. But at this point, the football games had not yet been canceled.

Gordon seemed impervious to all of it. In fact, Kathleen's arrival seemed to have filled him with national pride. In the face of gale force winds, he waxed poetic on his homeland. "For so long, the land was all we had," he said as we took in the pitch. "Our love for the land was written into our national anthem. *O Flower of Scotland, When will we see your like again, That fought and died for, Your wee bit Hill and Glen*. Every hill. Every glen. If the Scottish people had a piece of land of their own, they could make a life."

In Gordon's mind, this squall was no different than the last. He stood next to me, proud and strong, and leaned into the wind, an oak of a man, his roots dug deep into his native soil.

Then he saw something that made him think twice about the storm. "Look there, in the cove," he said, casually pointing to the horizon. "There's your sign that this *might* be serious. The freighters are seeking shelter."

I shielded my eyes with my hand and scanned the horizon. I could barely make out the shape of the massive shipping vessels that were lining up in a protected cove.

"When the sea captains decide to take shelter, that's gospel," Gordon admitted.

The combination of the concussive roar from the winds and the crashing sea and the heavy sky just absolutely murdered my senses. I breathed in the storm and breathed out an absolute nightmare. I didn't know how much more I could take. But I didn't want to look like a complete wuss in front of Braveheart in shorts. So I just stood there and let the winds tear me to shreds.

"Yes, this might be a serious storm after all," Gordon said, shrugging his shoulders.

Gospel it was. For the next forty-eight hours, the storm battered the Isle while I sheltered in the cabin. The winds made every single wood beam and board creak and moan. It felt like I was in the hull of a wooden ship that was on the verge of collapse. I thought again about the roofless house across the street. Now I had an all-too-real sense of what had happened to it.

In addition to being terrifying, the storm was mentally taxing. I cursed my luck: I'd traveled to the ends of the earth to watch football, but there would be no games played. This was the last stop of my trip. What would that mean for the book?

I spent my downtime in the cabin, where life became unnervingly ominous in the way of a horror movie. I was marooned out there in an alien landscape. I didn't have a car. The bus service was spotty. There was no town to walk to. There were no people to talk to. There was no pub nearby to gather in. There were no restaurants available. I only had a small bag of groceries that I was rationing. I was losing my mind.

Behind the cabin there was a short trail that led down to a loch. On the shore was a tiny shed with a bench inside. It did not have a door. For some unexplained reason, the winds did not reach this little shed, and it quickly became my only means of escape. At dusk, I walked down the path to the loch and sat alone in the shed and watched great curtains of sunlight sweep over the landscape in dramatic flashes. As my loneliness began to press in, I wondered if I had finally gone too far. At last, had I traveled too far from home?

But lucky for me, Gordon and Ollie continued to be some of the best tour guides I'd had for the entirety of my trip. Even without any games, Gordon and Ollie showed me the true beauty of island football.

They picked me up, and we started off driving through a part of the island where there were few humans but hundreds of grazing sheep set against hills of grass and heather. This was the most remote place I'd ever been. I had read that there were bogs on the isle that had been here for thousands of years. From the back-seat window of the car, it looked to me like the world had been stripped down to its barest elements. The level of desolate beauty was staggering, a place so wild and free and empty it was like a land before time. The landscape of lochs and mountains and dry-stacked stone walls—but very few trees or crops—rolled on until it dissolved into the sea. Beyond that was a horizon with nothing but sky and light and an emptiness so vast it broke my heart.

"You see those sheep out there?" Gordon asked, his stout brogue snapping my attention back. I realized I had been staring stupidly out the window like an old sugar-faced golden retriever. "You see how the sheep all have green lines marked on their wool?"

"Yeah," I said.

"The color the sheepherder marks his sheep often correlates to the football team he supports."

"Wait, what?" I asked.

"Those green lines on the sheep there mean that the sheepherder, he supports Celtic Football Club in Glasgow," Gordon said.

A little farther on, we came across a flock sprayed with blue and red dots. "That sheepherder supports Rangers Football Club in Glasgow," Gordon explained.

"This is fucking unbelievable," I blurted out before remembering, with horror, that Ollie was in the front seat. "Oh, I apologize for swearing!"

"That's okay," Ollie said.

"He's a Scottish lad," Gordon laughed. "He's heard much worse."

"I have," Ollie said.

"That sheepherder supports Aberdeen Football Club," Gordon said, pointing to sheep with red lines across their backs. "We may be just a little island. But we take football seriously here."

Gordon soon pulled into the Westside Football Club. The pitch was bordered by a single line of trees permanently arched over by the wind. A flock of sheep grazed behind a goal, and a short distance away was a battlefield cairn that marked a battle fought by the Lewis Clan in 1654 over territory and animals.

Gordon and Ollie told me about the Lewis and Harris Football League as we took in the pitch and Ollie dribbled the football that seemed to be permanently by his side. Formed in the 1930s, the league pits nine local clubs against one another in an annual competition. It's an amateur league and none of the players or coaches are paid. All the money from the tickets and concessions typically goes to the referees and linesmen. The league's season differs from the traditional September to May schedule on the mainland. This is due, of course, to the hostile weather of the Outer Hebrides. The teams on Lewis and Harris play during the long days of spring and summer. They're so far north that in June, they get up to eighteen hours of sunlight.

Our next stop was the Carloway Football Club, with a pitch set up against the North Atlantic Ocean. Gordon and Ollie told me that this place in particular was soaked endlessly by sheets of rain. If you put your laces through the ball at Carloway, you might also hit the Dun Carloway Broch, a round stone tower built around 200 BC, where island clans had taken shelter in trying times over the centuries.

After leaving Carloway, we drove down the road to the Calanais Standing Stones. This neolithic site of ten-foot-tall stones was built five thousand years ago, making it older than England's famous Stonehenge monument.

Up next was the wind-strafed Back Football Club. I've never in my life seen a windmill work as violently hard as it did at Back FC. There were tiny bus shelter–style team benches on the sideline that had had their plastic panels blown off. Immediately behind the benches was a dark and menacing bog, presumably full of lost balls and bodies. Supporters of Back FC stood in stands that had the aesthetics of an encampment in a zombie apocalypse movie.

After that we took a quick stop at Goat Hill: the closest thing I'd seen on this trip to a stadium, simply because it had a wrought iron gate with a name and symbol on it and a tiny concrete ticket booth. The ground was well tended to, because, Gordon said, "there's a man that lives in the park and takes care of it."

Small as these pitches were, it was clear that each one was the heart of the tiny village it was part of. They were places of communal glory and suffering and connection and belonging and identity. In a place so empty that the isolation was palpable, the local football pitches brought everyone together on spring and summer weekends.

The drive from the Lewis side of the island to the Harris side—home of the famous handwoven cotton cloth known as Harris Tweed—was a journey to a completely different planet. The rolling brown hills of Lewis dramatically gave way to jagged mountains. An old folk story said that a woman's silhouette could be seen in the mountain's ridgeline. She was lying down on her back, and the ancient ways spoke of a specific time in the year when the sunlight would shine straight through the Calanais Standing Stones to the woman's belly, marking a time of fertility. Once we were up on the winding road through the high pass of the mountains, I was shocked to find that they were covered in a green scape that reminded me of Maui, with turquoise-colored water below that looked like the Caribbean. We saw waterfalls and rainbows. It was truly mind-blowing.

At the end of all this beauty was the village of Tarbert, home to the Harris Football Club. They played on a pitch between the base of a mountain and the sea. There was a goal line that was so close to the water that errant balls went straight into the drink and had to be retrieved by supporters in kayaks. Then the balls were given to kids on the shore. This was where the kids became true Scottish footballers, because they had to then punt the balls over the tall fence in the face of driving winds and rain.

Our long day ended back on Lewis, at Lochs Football Club, the team that Gordon played for as a young man and where he is now vice president, kit man, and public relations director. As if that weren't enough, he is also coach of the U12 team, for which Ollie plays goalie.

The Lochs FC home pitch is called Creagan Dubh, which in Scottish Gaelic means "black crag." It was carved into an otherworldly landscape of peat and rock outcroppings and fields of windswept grasses. Immediately behind the goal was an exposed mound of dark earth and rock. It looked like a field used by hardy farmers who scratched out an existence on an inhospitable planet in the *Star Wars* universe.

As we toured the pitch, Ollie got out his football and took shots on goal. "There is no greater honor than to play for the place you come from," Gordon said, watching his son. "That's what this is all about for us here. To play for your village's youth team with the mates you've grown up with your whole life. Then you make your village's top club together and play in the Lewis and Harris Football League."

I was curious if Ollie would say the same thing. "What are your football dreams?" I asked him.

"To play for Lochs FC. The top club," he confirmed. "I want to play there with my friends and win a league cup. Then hopefully I can play for a proper team on the mainland like Ross County. Then I want to play for my country. I want to play for Scotland," he said.

Ollie continued to run and shoot. But the winds were really picking up. The ball often flew right back at him when he kicked it. His dogged efforts to play under these harsh conditions were a display of pure courage. There's an old adage in English football that says a player's true merit is measured not by his performance in Barcelona but on a cold and wet night in Stoke. Well, a cold and wet night in Stoke was child's play compared to the brutality of Scottish football on this island.

Ollie was head down, leaning into the wind, getting after it, for God and country and his little village. I could see that's what it was all about here. As we walked back to the car, Ollie squeezed in a few more dribbles. He was bright-eyed and his cheeks were flush.

As far as I was concerned, he was the very face of Scottish football.

My personal tour of the Isle of Lewis with Gordon and Ollie ended a day later in a village named Tolsta. It was one of the most remote places in the entire United Kingdom. All that was there was a tiny cluster of houses, a beach, and a cemetery where all the tombstones faced the sea. This was the only part of the Isle of Lewis that did not connect to any other part of the island. The B895 motorway terminated here, dead-ending in the middle of brown earth on one side and the sea on the other.

We parked at a turnaround near a beachhead. There were no other people. There were no other cars. There were no boats on the water. There were no birds. All that remained was the unrelenting wind. Down below, an endless set of waves that had traveled across the sea for hundreds of miles finally reached land and detonated on the shoreline.

As we drove back, we came upon a lone house that overlooked the sea. In the front yard, a football pitch had been cut into the earth. There were two nets and a single football. Even here at the fringe of the United Kingdom, at the end of the island, at the end of the road, dreams of football glory were still being born. All it took was a ball, an empty net, and the courage to keep kicking into the wind.

## CHAPTER SIXTEEN

# Stornoway, Isle of Lewis and Harris, Outer Hebrides, Scotland, April 7, 2024

The storm had mercifully died down a little bit. I was glad, because I had a football match to watch. Though it would be on television instead of in person, and not one of the Lewis and Harris League matches I had so hoped to see, it would be Scottish to the bone, and it had all the makings of a classic.

The rivalry between Celtic Football Club and Rangers Football Club is known as "the Old Firm," and is one of the most intense in world football, rivaling that of the fabled derby between Barcelona and Real Madrid. The teams are both based in Glasgow, only five miles apart from each other. As the marked sheep that Gordon had pointed out proved, the rivalry was felt just as deeply here on Lewis and Harris, almost three hundred miles away.

Celtic and Rangers are the most successful and popular clubs in Scotland and have consistently been the two top teams among the twelve that make up the country's top league, the Scottish Premiership. They have played each other 442 times in major competitions: Celtic have won 170 matches, Rangers 169 matches, and

103 ended in a draw. On the April Sunday of the match I was set to watch, they were locked into the Scottish Premiership's tightest title race in a decade. Whoever won would likely be crowned champion.

The intensity—and historical violence—of the rivalry comes down to the way the club's supporters divide themselves along sectarian and political lines. Rangers was founded in 1872 and draws its support from the Protestant population, particularly those of English and Scottish descent. Celtic was founded in 1888 by Irish Catholic immigrants. This game would take place at the Rangers stadium. I watched on the news as a militarized perimeter was secured around the stadium forty-eight hours before the match. Hundreds of riot police were called into action, and they mounted up like an army preparing for a siege upon their castle keep. This was even more striking given the fact that no Celtic supporters were even allowed to attend the match. The rule had been instituted to avoid bloodshed, though clearly the authorities deemed it insufficient on its own.

This segregation was also in effect on Lewis and Harris. As Gordon explained to me, I could not watch the match with him because he belonged to the official Isle of Lewis Rangers Supporters Club, and they had their own pub. Outsiders were forbidden from attending, especially an American from an Irish Catholic background like me.

I was instructed by Gordon to watch the match instead at the Stornoway Sea Angling Club. But first, he gave me a warning.

"Todd from America, before youse go there I need to tell youse a few things. The Stornoway Sea Angling Club is one of the only places open on Sunday for the match. It's also one of the only places in *Scotland* that allows both Celtic supporters and Ranger supporters."

"Oh," I said gravely.

"There are two floors. On the top floor are the Rangers supporters who, for one reason or another, don't watch the matches with us at the official supporters club where I go. Don't know what they did. But they are not with us."

That didn't sound great.

"The bottom floor hosts the official Isle of Lewis Celtic Supporters Club."

"Uh-oh," I said. "This keeps getting worse."

"Youse a smart lad, I know. Youse been with the East Enders and those Scousers in Liverpool. I know you got a head on you. But this is the *auld firm*. So, you just don't know how it will go. Things might go off."

As I waited for a cab to pick me up at the cabin and take me to the Stornoway Sea Angling Club, I looked up the Google reviews of the place. The first was a one-star review from 2023 that read: "When we visited it was all male, mostly playing pool and mostly intoxicated! (at 8pm) Had that sense that something was going to kick off! Especially when a local accused another local of cheating . . . we left promptly to the relative safety of our hotel . . . if you are local, enjoy pool, are male and enjoy the potential of a punch up . . . this is the place for you."

I was more than a little nervous as I got in the cab and started talking to John, the driver and a big jolly fella. He had a blue-eyed twinkle about him and a booming voice.

"Stornoway Sea Angling Club, aye. So, youse going to watch the *auld firm*, then?"

"Yes," I said, making sure not to say too much.

"Youse Celtic or Rangers, then?"

Back in Minneapolis, I'd asked a Scottish friend of mine about how to handle this exact question. "If anyone asks you if you support Celtic or Rangers," Deke McCallum told me, "your answer one hundred percent of the time is that you support Motherwell."

In the cab, I told John: "Motherwell."

"Aye, yeah, very well," he said, chuckling to himself. "Where youse from, then?"

"I'm Todd from America," I said. I told him about my love for English football and the Minnesota Kicks and Mike Bailey. "American sports don't have relegation or promotion," I explained. "When our teams are bad, nothing ever happens to them. They can just be bad forever."

"What's the fecking point, then? What youse playing for, then?"

"Trophies."

"Aye, there's always silverware to be won in America, isn't there," he said. "But relegation and promotion are real stakes. Gets you in a real fight."

For the rest of the cab ride, John told me fantastic stories about relegation and promotion for Scottish clubs with impeccable names: Hibernian, Hearts, Dumbarton. He told me about a lower-league club named Fort William that at one point didn't get a single victory in sixty-nine games and was labeled the worst team in the United Kingdom.

"Their pitch is at the base of Ben Nevis, the tallest mountain in Britain, and those lads lost every single game for years, and every day those lads were dealing with both of those mountains," John said, like the poet laureate of cabbies.

The car ride encapsulated everything that I'd wanted out of this entire trip. Brotherhood and banter, football madness, and good craic. There was a large part of me that wanted to ride around with John in that moment forever.

He pulled over in front of the Stornoway Sea Angling Club. It was a huge square building with a pitched roof, set right on the water, near the harbor. It looked like it hadn't seen an update since the 1980s. It had a few battered windows and a janky front door and gave off a serious roadhouse vibe.

I'd been entertained and distracted by John during the ride, but now I was worried again. John could tell.

"If you feel like things might go off, I want youse to leave immediately," John said, his voice tender and fatherly. "I've saved youse number in my phone. See here, it reads, 'Todd from America.' Ha! Now, that's my card there. If things start to go off or if someone starts asking you questions, I want you to leave."

"Okay," I said.

"Walk for ten minutes into town there. Nothing will be open except McNeil's pub. Go inside and order a pint. Then call me and I will come pick youse up when I can."

"Okay, thank you so much. I appreciate it, man."

"Have a good time, mate. I'm sure it will all be fine. I'll talk to youse soon."

I entered the club and walked up a flight of stairs. My plan was to watch the first half of the game upstairs with the blacklisted Rangers supporters, and the second half downstairs with the Celtic supporters. The upstairs bar had the vibe of a slapped-together man cave in the house of a newly divorced dad. It was sparsely decorated with beer signs. It had a few pool tables. A dozen Rangers supporters straight out of a police lineup of Union Loyalists stood around in a semicircle. They all gave me a quick once-over, but no one said hello or did so much as a head nod. Everyone just turned back to the giant screen and stared blankly at it. I found an empty side table and tried to shrink into the background.

One minute into the game, the veteran Celtic goalkeeper Joe Hart punted a long ball straight down the middle of the field that caught the Rangers defense completely off guard. It dropped perfectly into the path of speedy Celtic forward Daizen Maeda, and in one sequence he scooped up the long pass, sprinted down the field, and took a shot that ricocheted off the shin of the Rangers defender James Tavernier into the goal. The entire stadium, packed to the rafters with Rangers supporters, was stunned. Smoke from the pre-game pyrotechnics still wafted in the air and the banners were still getting raised.

On the second floor of the club, the jubilation coming from the Celtic supporters below was so palpable we could feel it like flames squeezing through the floorboards. They were screaming and cheering and tauntingly jabbing their pool cues into the ceiling. Stunned into an eerie silence, the Rangers supporters were almost immobile.

A half hour later, the score still 1–0, the second floor was unchanged. It was stone-cold quiet. Trying to blend in, not wanting to draw attention, I was still wearing my hat and jacket, and, reluctant to approach the bar, I hadn't even ordered anything. I could hear the nose hairs of the man next to me whistle every time he breathed out. No one was even drinking excessively; they just seemed angry and bitter.

In the thirty-fourth minute, Celtic were awarded a penalty. The team's sublime midfielder Matt O'Riley strolled up to the penalty spot and casually stroked the ball straight down the middle, easy as you like. The first floor became an inferno of jubilation. The cheering and applause poured through the floorboards again. The Celtic supporters started singing, and their voices climbed the walls of the entire building and engulfed the entire second floor.

Halftime couldn't have come soon enough. The moment the whistle blew, I stood up quietly, slunk to the staircase, and went to the first floor. I paid an admission at a check-in counter and entered a buzzing party of about seventy-five Celtic supporters, almost all of them in Celtic kits, moving every which way with cocktails in their hand. They were singing and swaying and shouting. They immediately welcomed me into the fold.

"Todd from America, what can I get you to drink?" a bald man with glasses asked.

"I'll take a Coke," I said.

"You a priest?" he asked, puzzled.

"Not a priest. Just not drinking at the moment."

"Aye," he said.

While he was off kindly getting me my Coke, a woman celebrating her sixtieth birthday came up to me. She had on a green sash and several beaded necklaces. "Todd from America, what can I get you to drink?" she asked.

"Oh, I've been sorted," I said. "That man at the bar is getting me a Coke."

"You a priest?" she asked.

"Haha, not a priest. Just not drinking at the moment."

"Aye," she said. "Would you like a pie?"

"Yes, oh my, yes," I said.

"Stay there, love."

She disappeared into a working kitchen off the bar where a woman was baking hand pies. A smell of baking bread and spiced meats wafted out. The woman returned and handed me a small hand pie in a little tin. It was warm and steamy.

"Here you go, love," she said.

"This is the greatest day of my life," I told her.

I bit into some buttery soft veg dancing in thick gravy. A piece of meat melted on my tongue. It was the single greatest bite of food during my entire trip. My face lit up.

This was the meat pie that I had dreamed about so long ago.

"There you go, love," she said, smiling.

"Can I buy you a drink?" I asked her. "For your birthday."

"No dear, I've had my fill," she said. "You just eat your pie. Match's about to start again."

The Celtic supporter came back with my Coke.

"A Coke for the priest," he said, handing me my glass.

"Cheers," I said, as we clinked glasses. "To Celtic Football Club."

In the fifty-fifth minute, James Tavernier, the Rangers defender who had gotten pantsed in the opening minute by Celtic forward Daizen Maeda, lined up for a penalty that he put into the top corner with authority. Finally, the sold-out Rangers home stadium crowd had something to celebrate—they waved Union Jacks, and above us, the drumming of feet came raining down. All the good craic and cheer around me disappeared. The Celtic supporters instantly sobered up and started chewing fingernails and yelling at the TV.

In the eighty-sixth minute, Rangers tied the game. The ceiling above us thundered like a stampede of buffalo. This was becoming an epic tilt, but somehow, I'd chosen the worst times to be on each floor, and it wasn't doing wonders for my nerves about where the whole night could be headed. Around me, dozens of heads sank to the tables. Arms were thrown back in disgust. Several men shot out of their seats, unable to even look at the Rangers supporters on TV celebrating the goal, and stormed out of the room.

Then, a minute later, Celtic substitute Adam Idah took a gorgeous pass from Paulo Bernardo that squeezed across the top of the Rangers' goal box between a thicket of Rangers defender legs, as if the ball had its own set of eyes. It arrived in Idah's stride. He took one step and swiveled, and the evasive move turned two Rangers defenders into each other like a scene from *Dumb and Dumber*. He slotted a low, hard shot right past the falling Rangers goalkeeper to give Celtic the lead again.

Finally, I was in the right place at the right time! The first floor of the club erupted in one of the most emotionally explosive displays I had seen on my trip. Grown men shot off their seats and began blindly running around the room in hysterics. Clusters of men hugged each other in religious rapture. In seconds, the room filled with song. The voices of the Celtic supporters caught fire once again. Someone handed me another Coke and someone else handed me another pie. It was a true privilege to be an eyewitness to the pure glory and exhilaration that this beautiful game can give its supporters.

The ref added three minutes of injury time. In the ninety-second minute, Rangers midfielder Rabbi Matondo took a pass on the side of the goal box. He took a couple of dribbles, deftly sidestepped a few Celtic defenders, then threw down a hammer strike on goal. In the exact second that Matondo struck the ball, every single Celtic supporter in the room froze. Matondo's shot struck inside the top corner of the goal and daggered the heart of every one of them. By the time Celtic goalie Joe Hart scooped the ball out of his goal, I had already left the building. It was as pure an Irish goodbye as there ever will be. No salutations. No goodbyes. No handshakes. No words. Just gone.

I walked ten minutes into town and entered the safe confines of McNeil's pub and ordered a pint, as instructed by John. It was the last drink of my journey. I didn't want to celebrate how far I'd traveled with an American soda. This called for a proper pint. A man in his sixties with a wind-bitten, rosy face sat at the end of the bar. He wore a tattered seaman's sweater and read a crumpled newspaper. His small dog was curled up sleeping on a large rucksack at the base of his bar stool. A dark pint with a perfect creamy head stood at attention on a coaster in front of him. He set the newspaper down and glanced up at the Real Madrid vs. Manchester City Champions League match on the television. Then he picked up the pint. The warm and soothing glory of the first sip burst across his face like a sunrise. I took a sip of my pint, too. We silently nodded at each other. Two fellow travelers in a moment of respite.

Months earlier, I had climbed to the top of the Spurs stadium with Murph. Now, after those two and a half months and thousands of miles, McNeil's pub in Stornoway on the Isle of Lewis and Harris was the last stop on my trip. Tomorrow, I had a flight off the island to Edinburgh and then to London and then finally to Minneapolis.

I scrolled through the day's football headlines. There were just a few weeks left in the English football season. England and Scotland were now rife with stories of relegation and promotion. In every corner of the United Kingdom, communities were hanging on the precipice of their team going down or going up. I kept scrolling on my phone. I fell down the rabbit hole once again.

The Black Cats of Sunderland were now calling out to me, a football siren luring this wayward supporter to the Stadium of Light in the northeast of England. There was a bitter relegation battle in Scottish football's League Two between Bonnyrigg Rose FC and Forfar Athletic FC. There was an upcoming match in an old Scottish mining town that began to tickle the creative part of my mind. In English football's National League, Boreham Wood and Dorking Wanderers and Kidderminster were in a three-way relegation battle at the bottom of the league table. A visit to Kidderminster would give this book a poetic chance to come full circle. Imagine the possibilities! I could finally visit the Museum of Carpet!

My fever for this game flushed clear through me, soaking my entire body and mind. It overpowered my rational thinking and common sense. Within seconds, I was looking at a map and charting a course to more games and towns. I deliriously studied a vast network of interconnected trains and planes and buses and boats. These railways and highways and seaports were the UK's central nervous system, delivering football supporters and all the pain and ecstasy that this game brings into every part of the region. A myriad of details flashed before me: calling Sarah, calling my boss, changing flights, booking new trains and new hotels. I scribbled a flurry of notes.

Then the dog sleeping on the floor of the pub loudly snort-sneezed, and it broke the spell that English football had cast over me. Suddenly, I was back in my body. Back in reality. I could only sit there and laugh at myself. My lunacy to keep carrying on down the road meant that I was officially a proper football supporter. Being a proper supporter of English football didn't mean that I simply supported a specific club and went to matches. It meant that I was now on a journey without an end.

The century-old format of relegation and promotion makes English football live forever in the hearts of its supporters. It links all the teams, in all the leagues, in all the years, and because of this, the history of the game spirals back and forth across the face of time. It stretches across seasons and generations of supporters in every neighborhood and city and town and landscape where football is played. Each new season in English football has real stakes, wins and losses and draws that affect the team and the towns and their past and present and future. Every season, teams go up and teams go down. An eternal cycle of birth and death.

There will be more English football games in my future, for sure. There will be more grounds to visit, more moments of wonder to drink in, and more pies to eat. The game was inside me now and would not be denied. But it was time for this trip to end. I took a celebratory sip from my pint. Then I called John for a ride home.

# May 2025

I'm in the basement staring at the map of England taped to the wall next to my desk. More than a year removed from the trip, the names and places and football clubs on the map are no longer abstract destinations shimmering in my dreams. They have moved off the map and into my real life. To quote my spirit guide Bilbo Baggins, I've gone "there and back again."

There are new additions to the basement wall. Above the map is a quote from Henry Rollins, lead singer of the eighties-era punk band Black Flag: "I don't have talent, I have tenacity, I have focus. I know, without any delusion, where I come from and where I can go back to." To the right of the map of England are thirteen pieces of construction paper in a rainbow of colors. On each piece of paper, I've written the name of a chapter or short story. I've found it easier to mentally and physically manage the writing of this book by compartmentalizing the work into small, individual bites, like fun-size candy bars. To the left of the map, there is a poster Murph gave me featuring the giant smirking face of Danny DeVito. It serves as a constant reminder of the absurd fact that I pulled this whole thing off.

The trip still doesn't seem real.

That is because the book grew out of my lowest point as a writer. None of this was possible just a short while ago. I had sent out dozens of query letters to editors and literary agencies in New York, Los Angeles, and London and was soundly rejected for months on end.

Then, as in all great stories of relegation and promotion, I received a minor miracle. My own relegation math finally worked in my favor. On a random Sunday night, I received two nibbles from two agents at literary firms in New York City. They both loved my query letter and set up interviews to talk.

In the first interview, the agent asked me a simple question: "What ties all the teams and towns in this book together?" I embarrassingly could not answer the question and ultimately bombed the first interview. Two days later, I had a second chance.

I was at work at Hiawatha Supply when Tim Wojcik from the Levine Greenberg Rostan Agency called me. As we chatted, I sat in a folding chair in a storage room I refer to as "the Panic Room" because it's a secluded, windowless bunker filled with tools and supplies. As fate would have it, Tim asked me the same exact question—word for word—as the first agent. But this time I'd done my homework and had an answer. I talked passionately about relegation and promotion and how the feeling of hope in football and in life ties the clubs and towns together.

My courage to carry on as a writer roared back in that moment. I spoke confidently about all the storylines I was already chasing in the UK and all the contacts I had made.

I was so desperate to sign with Tim and the LGR Agency and sell my book proposal that I decided at that moment to put aside all pretenses and literary airs. My writing life was in injury time. So, I went for promotion right then and there, and I spoke directly and honestly about my reality and why it made me the right man to write this book at this time.

"I know what it feels like to be relegated," I said bluntly. "I don't write full-time. I only write as a side hustle. I work full-time as the yard boss at a landscape supply store named Hiawatha Supply. We sell bulk landscape supplies. We are also a disposal site. So, yeah, man, I literally work at a dump. I'm actually talking to you from a room full of shovels."

"A room full of shovels," Tim repeated. "*Who* are you?"

The answer to that question was ultimately the start of my transformation from the sad, middling writer I had become into "Todd from America," an alter ego filled with the courage to plow headfirst into the foreign world of English football. This transformation became one of the greatest feats of my life.

During the brutal slog it took to write this book while working full-time, I found my motivation from those I had met along my journey. I owed it to all of them. I needed to match the religious devotion shown by the Everton supporters; the snark and humor of Mark and Jase in Grimsby; the grit of Jimmy toiling away on the docks; the brotherhood of the Freestylers; the northern soul of Jack and Andrei in the cages of Manchester; the strength to fight on, headfirst into the wind, demonstrated by Ollie on the Isle of Lewis; the stamina of the away supporters in the driving rain in Hartlepool; the wild heart of the Last True King of Scotland in Edinburgh; the spirit of rebellion at the Old Spotted Dog; the thunder of the song and chant of the Wolves supporters; the heart of Dave and Reg in Stockport; and, more than anything, the work ethic of Peter Clarke preparing the pitch by the North Sea.

For the last year and a half, I had worked Monday to Friday at Hiawatha Supply during the day and written at night. I only gave myself Friday night off. On Saturday and Sunday, I rose at 5:30 a.m. and wrote from 6:30 a.m. to 10:30 a.m. Then I went back to bed from 10:30 a.m. to 11:30 a.m. I woke up, had lunch, and drank copious amounts of caffeine. I wrote from 12:30 p.m. to 3:00 p.m. In the late afternoons, I would reconnect with Sarah and Murph and perform my marital and parental obligations. (Yes, I grilled all the chicken.) After dinner, I did light editing from 7:00 p.m. to 8:30 p.m. to set myself up for the next day. I was asleep by 9:15 p.m. There were no vacations or writing retreats or workshops or sabbaticals from this schedule.

The only way forward was through.

Now, as I sit at my writing desk, I look over one last time at the map on the wall. I realize with acute joy and sadness that this epilogue is the final story in my journey. Although I dream that I can continue to do this, to make "Todd from America" a series, to explore more places in world football, I know the odds are stacked against me.

I know, without any delusion, where I come from and where I am going back to.

Suddenly, I see the overhead basement lights flicker on and off. I wear soundproof headphones and listen to instrumental tracks by the Beastie Boys when I write, so I'm wrapped in a cocoon of sensory deprivation. The flickering lights are the signal that Sarah would like to come downstairs to chat. I remove my headphones.

"Come on down," I say.

Sarah walks down the basement stairs and sits on the step adjacent to my desk. She's been outside gardening, wearing a huge sun hat favored by field laborers and the gardening smock I bought for her at a botanical garden I visited in Scotland. She is as golden as ever.

"How's the writer in residence?" she asks, laughing. The band of landscaping miscreants I work with jokingly gave me that moniker at Hiawatha Supply, because it is believed that I am the only writer in Minneapolis who also works at a dump.

Sarah and I catch up as married couples do. We chat in quick succession about the week ahead, work schedules, plans and appointments, our aging parents, and any updates about Murph.

After the essentials have been covered, Sarah stands up and gets ready to go back upstairs and into the bright summer sun. She looks down at me. Her eyes are filled with compassion. Then she says the two words every struggling artist and worker and football supporter needs to hear when they are fighting for their lives, when they are fighting off relegation.

"Keep going."

# ACKNOWLEDGMENTS

This book would not be possible without the following people.

Thank you to my family. Sarah Ann Schneider Smith, my dearest Sass, you joked once that you wished you'd married a man with a useful skill set like carpentry, but instead you married a writer. After twenty-four years of marriage and counting, that is still hilarious. You're still saddled with a man whose only true skill is daydreaming. But without your love and sense of humor none of this is possible. Murphy Smith, being your dad is the single greatest highlight of my life, a continuous Kun Agüero at 93:20. Our good hangs after I finished long days at this were oftentimes my only solace from the madness that engulfs me when I'm writing. I'm forever grateful for our bond. Thank you to my parents, Gary and Linda Smith, for never giving up on me, for taking me to the Washburn Child Guidance Center, for hiring a battalion of tutors to keep me academically afloat so long ago. Most important, thank you for allowing to me the freedom to move west to Missoula, Montana, to find my own path, a journey that remarkably has resulted in three books. Thank you to Elliot, Olivia, and Addie for always filling Smith family dinners with a chorus of laughter; to my father-in-law, William Schneider, for bringing some much-needed class and style to my life. I am a shirtless and silly seventh-inning Harry Carey to your Fred Astaire, and I love it. Thank you to the Wright family, Jane and Terry and Kat and

John, for supporting me and letting me blather on and on at your family gatherings; to all my relatives in Iowa—your encouragement and enthusiasm for my writing is always a shining light; and to my brother, Tony, and sister, Becky, for, well, everything. Being your idiot brother is simply the best.

Thank you to my team: To my agent, Tim Wojcik, and everyone at the Levine Greenberg Rostan Agency for believing in me and this project even before I fully did. Tim, you were the hard-charging Stevie G spirit that I needed, and I will be forever grateful for your hard work in helping me get out of a life of relegation. To Mia Robertson at Gallery Books for your early encouragement and support for this project. Your passion and championing of this book was amazing from the beginning. To my editor, Max Meltzer, for being a late-game substitution; your guidance and endless work on my dodgy manuscript was truly amazing. It was your narrative vision that moved this book from the ninth tier to promotion. And to Hanna Preston for your editorial insight and encouragement; you gave me the lift I needed when I needed it the most.

Thank you to the writers in my life: To Chris Clayton—you are the best editor in the Twin Cities, and your editorial eyes on the early pages of the book proposal and sample chapter were as delicious as the pho at the Hmong Village. After all our years of working together, I still love being in our two-man Pavement-style writing duo. To Dana Raidt for the humorous snark about our ridiculous lives as writers. To John Branch, the best writer I know and a dude cooler than Fat Lever, our friendship continues to be one of the highlights of my writing career. To Adam Wilson for being my mensch. And to Chris Jones and Wright Thompson and

Steve Rushin and S.L. Price; although we've never met, all your long-form narrative nonfiction about the sport of football and your general dudeness have always been my North Star.

Thank you to Hannah Harlow, owner of The Bookshop of Beverly Farms, in Beverly, Massachusetts. You are the single best friend a writer could ever have. It was your kindness and little bookstore that helped me stay in the writing game when I wanted to quit. I will be forever grateful for your friendship and the gems your store sent me to keep my creative spirit alive.

Thank you to all the people in my work life; none of this is possible without your support and understanding: to Steele and Nan Arundel for allowing me to chase a dream; to all my coworkers at Landscape Love and Hiawatha Supply for your dogged support of my side hustle and for stepping up while I was away; and to everyone in the Weiner Wednesday Nation.

Thank you to Luca Gunther and John Munson; our time together in Wales and Liverpool was life-changing. Thank you to Jim McGuinn for joining me on part of this journey; our time wandering around in the wilds of Scotland was truly inspiring. And to Deke McCallum for all the advice and friendship as I planned this impossible journey; I am so thankful for our brotherhood.

Thank you to my people: To the Downey family, Ann and Dave and Cee and Liam and Owen; your stream of GIFs and lunch dates were a lifeline during the entirety of the writing process. To the Simitis family, Matt and Laurie and Jody and Tess; your funny texts and sports chirping always brought me back to reality after long days in the writing hole. To the Rauen family, Paul and Becca and Teddy and Bay; thank you for not making St. Paul boring. Paul, you are my Maldini on the back line on the pitch and off. To the Prentice family, Ann and Steve and Oliver and Matilda; our time together navigating the absurd world of youth sports made up some of the best years of my life. To Leif and Heidi Haugen; you have always been there for me during the various stages of my writing career, and I sincerely appreciate it. To the entire Vance family for making my soccer addiction seem normal compared to yours. And to Dawn Mitchell, for your kindness and friendship and for always including me in the Twin Cities sports media world.

Thank you to the following people for helping me get through such a punishing work and writing schedule: Johannes Butscher and Sam Erickson—our meals at the Animales food truck on Friday nights talking about football and Fullkrug and Freiburg were a source of pure joy; Paul Spring for being the single greatest singer-songwriter-snowplowman I've ever had the pleasure to rip through the night with; Morris Weintraub for your enthusiasm and excitement during the early stages of this book project; Bones McInnis and Moondog Fuenffinger, you are my brothers in the struggle; Donny Donowitz and Thomas Meagher for listening as I workshopped these stories verbally; Brown Bear, Bergie, Slick Rick, and The Microwave for our constant text thread about football that is as greasy as Adama Traoré's arms; Stephanie Harris and Carl Wodele for being real ones; Wooly Nelson and Margie Houlihan for always asking how the writing was going and meaning it; Scout Sagsveen for always taking a time-out to laugh; Betsy Chastain for being my loudest cheerleader; Fernando and Edmundo for all the tacos and football talk; the Black Dew Crew for all your cured meats and dewskis; Michael Robole for riding shotgun as I drove to Chicago to interview Idles—I could not have asked for a better wingman to start this journey; Lorne Petkau and

Jeff Hoeppner for all the sports chatter; Sophia Petrillo for being as annoyed about everything as I am; Eliza Bean for all our inspiring talks about what it means to live as a working artist; Alicen Burns for being the single greatest supporter of books and writing; Potter!; Chris Pavlich and the band Two Harbors—I began each writing session by listening to your song "Brothers and Sisters" and it always put me in the right place every single time; tell it, Deszczowa Wiedzma, for helping me navigate all the land mines that occur in my life of balancing my art and labor—I sincerely appreciate our friendship; the *SmartLess* podcast and the *Men in Blazers* podcast for being my companions as I went for long walks and tried to sort all of this out; and the Donkey Soccer League, a starting XI of all Morris Buttermakers, for all your tireless support and for filling my life with glory and misery in equal measure.

Thanks to the people I met along my long road through the UK: To the Bailey family, Andrew and Lorna and Phoebe and Lucy; your friendship and hospitality gave me a home overseas. To Mick Allchin and James Briggs and Sukhdev Johal and Ric Riscardo at Clapton Community Football Club for welcoming me into your revolution. To all the Scousers I met in Liverpool for letting me step into your football-mad world; I will always appreciate our time together. To the Freestylers, endless thanks for letting me join your squad. To Jack Bies and Andrei Valimareanu in Manchester for your kindness and for passing me the ball even though you didn't really want to. To Footy Addicts for making football accessible for everyone. To Graeme Giles for your guidance through the landscape of Scottish football. To everyone at *The Cod Almighty* and Rock Community Food Bank in Grimsby. To Brad Seymour in Bury; your kindness and hospitality at the

Bury Football Club is a shining example of what makes lower-league football so wonderful. To Dave Marchbank and all the lads in Stockport; I entered the pub as a stranger and left a Hatter forever. To Gordon and Ollie Greenhowe; your tour of the Isle of Lewis and Harris was a perfect way to end the book. Slainte! To Peter Clarke in Arbroath for being the Boomer of the Northeast. And to Adam Devonshire and Jon Beavis from Idles for your encouragement and inspiration to take on this project.

To those I lost along the way: Pappy Kern for being the first person in my life to tell me that I could be a writer, ironically as we plowed snow together; and to Kim Brown, Katherine Noland, Gaga Feinberg, Adam Yauch, and Jay Mathews for being the stars that have helped light my way through this world.

## ABOUT THE AUTHOR

**Todd Smith** is the director of a landscape supply yard in South Minneapolis and the author of two books: *Hockey Strong: Stories of Sacrifice from Inside the NHL* and *Brave Enough*, cowritten with Olympian Jessie Diggins. Smith runs the Donkey Soccer League, a Sunday-morning game for assorted nitwits and out-of-shape, middle-aged scalawags.